Contents

Acumen would like to thank the sponsor
who made this anthology possible, but who wishes
to remain anonymous.

The anthology is dedicated to all the readers and
contributors throughout the past twenty five years
who have made the continuity of the journal possible.

Thanks are also due to the magazine's co-editors,
Danielle Hope, William Oxley and Glyn Pursglove, for
their valuable work and inputs into the magazine over the
years.

Notes from the Editor

Reading through sixty issues of *Acumen,* has been a privilege. All the poems published have much to recommend them, and it was difficult to make the choices for this volume.

However, reading the poems was not just a nostalgic journey through 25 years of editing, but I felt like I was reading a social history of the past quarter of a century. And not just a social history, but a history of poetic forms and fashions. When I first began *Acumen,* underlying the eternal themes of poetry (which according to T.S. Eliot are birth copulation and death), there seemed to be in many submissions a searching for role-models: grandparents in particular, especially those who had fought in the Wars and upheld firmer traditional values of life, were extolled and acknowledged often with a hint of sadness and nostalgia. A looking back to what almost seemed a more caring and gentle age.

But over the next few years all this changed and current concerns crept into the submissions and finally took them over: poverty, violence, mental illness, boredom with life; and all still coupled with more-than-merely-competent poems on how beautiful this world can be, on love (though a little too often on lost love as the century went on). And the poems themselves began to change. The long sprawling free verse poems became stricter, form and rhyme slid back into the lines, the personal poem came to be the norm to such an extent that if a poet wrote a fiction with the poem, it was taken as true.

Then came 9/11 and poetry changed again, almost overnight. Global visions were expressed, anger and hurt and bewilderment burst into the poetry. And suddenly questions appeared: about God; war; where had we gone wrong; the death of love; and what was each individual's relationship with the other. Nature was seen more often now within the lines, a Wordsworthian Nature – even if not spelt with a captial N – often doubling for the lost faiths, or taking faith to new and different levels. It was an exciting read of the first sixty issues.

But after two years and many reads and choices, the following poems were decided upon. Then came more decisions: how to order them, present them to the readers. There are many ways of presentation in an anthology: chronologically, alphabetically, by theme, etc. I chose the first: and the poems presented here are more or less in the order in which they were originally printed in *Acumen*. I say more or less, for there have been a few minor shifts to enable a longish poem to appear on left hand/ right hand pages so as not to break the continuity by having to turn over in the middle of a reading. My one regret was being unable to include, for copyright reasons, poems that had appeared in *Acumen* by Samuel Beckett and Elizabeth Jennings.

In keeping with the policy of the magazine, there are no biographical notes attached at the end. While giving me a few extra pages for poems here, the main reason why there have never been such notes in *Acumen* is because I have always thought the poem was the most important item. If it needed biographical notes to become accessible, or to have a deeper meaning then, to me, it failed as a poem. And I have to say that in many places where notes *about* the poet have been appended, these have often become more read than the poems. Most readers will have access to a computer, either at home or in the library, for more information one can 'google' the poet, *but preferably only after finding out about them first by reading the poem.*

As well as publishing poetry, *Acumen* has published prose, interviews with poets on their poetry, reviews; has produced Focus Sheets for Readers in which one poet had between six and eight poems in a poster-sized insert; looked at poets of the past and re-evaluated them; assessed well-known poets of the present; and had poems in translations from eminent translators. I have also done minimal commissioning in order to keep opportunities for publiation as open-ended as possible, as one of the most important imperatives for a grant-aided magazine is to give maximum opportunity for new poets to find publication.

But poetry is *Acumen's raison d'être,* and here is a personal choice of what I consider some of the best poems of the previous 25 years.

Patricia Oxley, Brixham, 2010

Dannie Abse

The Abandoned

Du, Nachbar Gott ... – R.M. Rilke

...thy absence doth excel
All distance known – George Herbert

1.
God, when you came to our house
  we let you in. Hunted,
    we gave you succour,
      bandaged your hands,
        bathed your feet.

Wanting water we gave you wine.
Wanting bread we gave you meat.

Sometimes, God, you should recall
  we are your hiding-place.
    Take away these hands
      and you would fall.

Outside, the afflicted pass.
  We only have to call.
    They would open you
      with crutch and glass.

Who else then could we betray
  if not you, the nearest?
    God, how you watch us
      and shrink away.

2.
Never have we known you so transparent.
You stand against the curtain and wear

its exact design. And if a window opens
(like a sign) then is it you
or the colours that are blown apart?
As in a station, sitting in a carriage,
we wonder which of the waiting trains depart.

God, you can't help your presence
any more than the glassy air that lies
between tree and skies. No need to pass
through wave-lengths human ears can't sense.

We never hear the front door close when you are
                                        leaving.
Sometimes we question if you are there at all.
No need to be so self-effacing;
quiet as language of the roses
or moss upon a wall.

We have to hold our breath to hear you breathing.

3.
Dear God in the end you had to go.
Dismissing you, your absence made us sane.
We keep the bread and wine for show.

The white horse galloped across the snow,
melted, leaving no hoofmarks in the rain.
Dear God, in the end you had to go.

The winds of war and derelictions blow,
howling across the radioactive plain.
We keep the bread and wine for show.

Sometimes what we do not know we know –
in Armageddon town they write your name
dear God. In the end you had to go.

Yet boarding the last ship out we'd sorrow
that grape is but grape and grain is grain.
We keep the bread and wine for show.

Will world be leased to vulture and the crow?
Small lights upon the shore begin to wane.
Dear God in the end you had to go,
we keep the bread and wine for show.

4.

They say, truant, you've vanished, address unknown,
that those who trusted you don't do so now
and, like the bereaved, feel empty and alone.

No wonder the plaudits for you grow fainter:
the George Herbert-like poems; the holy
plagiarism of each landscape painter.

And the congregations fewer for the sting of prayer,
all the fawning words, all the honeyless hum –
all for you, neighbour Gott. And you not there.

Still we call the Register. You're not excused.
Disease? Here sir. *Famine?* Present sir. *War?*
They say you fashioned us so who's accused?

5

Last night, awakened, did we hear you call?
Memory, father of tears, who was that knocking?
That incautious noise. Was there someone knocking?
Someone we once knew when we were small?

God, you have so many disguises. Once, we
from our dark bedroom cots, in mild fear,
could see how across the walls and ceiling
shadows of light would appear and flee.

This morning an omen downstairs on the floor,
a fallen picture frame. No homecoming,
no shadow of a shadow returning to stay,
no slow opening of a creaking door.

And our thoughts blank as an angel's mirror
since you, it seems, have travelled the other way
farther than all distance known, and further.

1957, 2008

Philip Gross
Hearing Voices

Stones speak, truer than us.   Give me the clear
chapel bass of a granite house above the sea,
the burr of sandstone, or a slate-flagged floor
tuning itself to footsteps...Yet I'm sat here,
buttonholed by bricks and mortar with their eighty
year old gossip I can't catch or quite ignore.

(What did the doctor say? What happened in the end?)
I thought: I'll strip one room to quietness.
It peeled in whispers.   Melancholic brown, a fuss of
paisley, nursery pink, like tones of voice a friend
or widower would spot in a crowd, years later: yes, that's her,
it wasn't what she said...Deciduous

mulched tatters, clogging underfoot. Me, me –
my blade grates plaster.   It calls up the taste
of dereliction, bashed-out walls with skin-
deep patchwork opened to the sky, our curiosity,
the wrecking ball.   My smug new paper waits.
Sweep up the dead.   (Then how shall I begin?)

William Oxley

Spring Night

Spring night; night without suffering
Black, mottled with stars
Peace's infinite clinging
And all the time fumes of love rising
Like scent over wet meadows.
Nothing that man does really mars
The far smiling shadows
And infinite silences,
So burst open the brittle windows
That are suburbia's cell bars
And let in the essences,
For more than death tongues the night air
And awaits you out there.

Dinah Livingstone

Woman in a Dressing Gown

On the keen edge of morning
she does not dance,
no angel, more of a mist drifting.
In what sense does she exist?
A noise of passions ringing her for dead:
she can't get dressed.

She takes tea back to bed,
covets more rest.
Unshod, ungirded, unsafe fuzzy head,
she senses both at once
why Anthony disarmed for dying,
Cleopatra dressed.

Katherine Gallagher

November, Bois de Vincennes

I listen to autumn's
wild festivity caught in every leaf
as trees gather colour
and leaves burn to their centres –
bonfires across the earth.

All summer has been winding down
to this: the blaze, a dance,
a requiem for the year's leaves;
a fire subsumed into stillness
guarding an inner music,
a flute-voice echoing
again and again towards newness –
spring's first twist of season,
its sheltering braids of green.

Michael Croshaw
A Prayer for Playing Children
Written after hearing children sing
'Brown Girl in the Ring' on park-swings.

Sing, children, sing!
Don't swing down from your afternoon heights
for anyone, or anything.
Swing high on those dream-branched metal trees that carry you
as in celestial chariots to the sun.
Behind you city-grimaced faces wait,
the depleted, the defeated,
money-grabbers, worriers whom
your song must overwing.
You must still be stars when they are dust,
their lust, which you vaguely understand,
crumpled in the tall light of your shining.
So many girls will leave that flashing ring
of haloed time you sing of.
So many plums disgorge a sugary sweetness
to bring to last decay and sleep the dalliers
who cannot save from markets their song-coins gleaming.
But you must guard your childhood – guide of evening,
night's still-folding, day-grid holding warm –
your songs of fly-away, and grace, and youth,
preserve from bleak-tongued, hungry-mouthed marauders
who would grind for their better meal your living truth.

Katherine Gallagher

Song for an Unborn

Child, curled in the night
I call you, know you
feeling your way against the walls.
You are so used to darkness now –
your blind busy limbs
buffet and push, quickening
as you weigh yourself and float.

In the beginning, I ran through hours
trying to feel you real.
Daily I bargained with you,
was cajoled and soothed
by your moves, winning,
always teaching me. And yesterday
you set yourself on X-ray, vividly
thumb in mouth, head down, a plunderer
looping in the sky.

Half-afraid with new happiness
I scanned that picture,
hunting details – your face, body,
you.   Suddenly I knew
your eyes were almost ready
to lift the dark.

Berenice Moore

After the Crash

They say life must go on;   although you died
I am unscarred and I shall soon be well.
My grievous hurt is more than they can tell:
half of my self is riven from my side.

I live again the moment when you cried
my name and God's as if you could repel
the monstrous Juggernaut or could compel
some power to intervene, turn death aside.

If, after all, there should be something more
than lilies, roses trodden into clay:
green fields and sunlight, brightness in the air
beyond the confines of the corridor
that separates our night time from our day,
can I find comfort, thinking of you there?

Graham Mort

The Herb Grower

He was station master here nineteen years,
Until the line began to die, train by train;
Steamers turned to diesal and his heart shrank
One beat each time he turned his ear
To the gradient below the station.

First the night-trains ceased, but dream-trains
Hammered sleep into the old pattern;   he heard
Them pass in the unlit bedroom, hooting like owls
Under flaming funnels and fire-boxes.

Then days too dragged empty of passengers and freight,
Until three trains a day proclaimed his poverty.

He retired and the station became a mere halt,
A platform in the fields, where few passengers
Got on or off, where travellers cast a listless
Glance, half curious between cities.

He stayed on at the station-house, tending
His herb garden in sight of the track, unbending
His back from the trowel each time he hears
The drumming of wheels, returning a wave
From some railman serving out his time
In the same memories.

Now he raises slow plants, rosemary
And thyme, sages, marjorams and mints,
Pressing them into pots, as each morning
He pressed rich flake into his briar
To meet the mail-train, flicking open the lid
Of his father's watch to mark lateness or punctuality.

His seedlings and cuttings take hold
In soil shaken by a century of trains;
Their roots touch into his dreams, heavy
Aromas from their leaves mingle with soot
From the panting locomotives, spreading
Over his sleep as over a grave.

Roy Fuller

Amatory Dreaming in Old Age

I dream you've left me.   And what can bring you back?
For I am as I am;   you as you were –
I've nothing to offer beauty, not even rape.
My heart, my entire being's sick, for there's
No chance time or the world will change my lot.

I wake, and wonder if phantom vanishing still
Implies my jealousy (at some suave god
Handling the tender flesh I thought I owned)
Or, worse, prefigures death, the final wound
Inflicted by the capricious female will.

Philip Gross
A Chess Piece

A chandelier hangs like a flounce of fountain spray
arrested in mid fall.   Beneath, dry vulture-necked
old men are ranked, eyeball to eyeball, tête-à-tête.
A hundred clocks tut-tut their precious time away.

It's called a Congress but it's war.   It's like Versailles
nineteen-nineteen.   Facing this season's prodigy,
a grave pale schoolboy, the retiring champion feels
the drag of history.   The books hold no reply

to that blue-eyed blank computer-innocence
(The parents say 'Sometimes we wonder where he came
from.   He eats, sleeps and dreams the game...
But he's our boy.') nor to the bleak Modern Defence
– king deeply bunkered, bishop in a fianchetto
sheathed in pawns, snug as a warhead in its silo.

William Oxley
The Phoenix and the Woman

Out of the blinding, the intolerable, the fruitful sun
That nest of the golden-feathered Phoenix
The shapely vision of life somehow emerges
And in men's breasts is reduced to ashes.

The young hold hands awhile and then grow stale
And only the sun and the prophets rebuke them.
But in me the silent rage of love goes on
And the endless struggle with dreary time.

Every day the painful renewal of vision,
Every day the empire of money grows
And the futile procreation of stones
That leave me a nomad in a desert of shame.

It is hard to get used to being poet and lover
When the shiver of pleasure animates time
And every damn fool is a cankered navel
And God's shut away in a dictionary of death.

But she said: 'Let your integrity protect
The spirit from waste, my phoenix of fury,
I will be your cool bride of flame
And exquisite moon to your troubled sun.'

Then in imagination history like a photograph burned
And I saw the coals of eternity glow under me,
As at the words of a loving woman
My shabby bird, fresh plumed, flew back to the sun.

Richard O'Connell
North

Nobody sleeps. Up here in summer time
the naked sunlight hammers on your skull
so fierce you can't stay out in it for long –
till like the town you end up slumped in dark
and smoke at the gigantic Gateway Bar.
Brash kids crowd in, all headed for the mines,
red-faced as infants – hungry innocents.
Old roustabouts sit silent in their chairs:
they're iced in still – wedded to night and cold
and murder undetected. Which hasn't killed
with gun or knife or maybe with bare hands?
The frozen lakes lock secrets in their skulls.

While Eskimos chaw beer like so much blubber
at the back tables – grinning Genghis Khans –
ferocious in their furs and moon-pocked faces,
a waitress shivers like a tropic fish
among barbed glances – chilled down to her marrow.
I swallow my sixth or seventh glass of beer
watching the Go-Go Girl from Winnipeg
baring her boyish torso to the bold
applause of fists and stomping feet Go! Go!
Only the waiters slinging trays of foam
in rolled shirt-sleeves, seem in touch with the real
and most of all the owner 'Baby Face'
perched high, impassive as a totem god.

Wearily I climb to bed, not even drunk,
collapsing in bright daylight. Wide awake
I sob an endless dream of loss and death.

Carole Satymurti
Desk

We'd call, 'Hootie. Hootie."
and he'd fling wide
his study window, stand
royal, framed in black.
I remember him sun-lit,
smoke from his pipe blossoming
slow into the still air,
always mock stern

until, laughing suddenly,
he'd reach behind him
opening, we knew,
the top drawer of his desk
where Important Work was done,
then – an arc of barley sugar,
humbugs, butterscotch,
largesse to scramble for.

For thirty years, I've written
in the shadow of this desk: its
space for a vase of philadelphus,
fossils, papers generously spread ...
Often I've looked for,
failed to find a desk as big
with drawers as deep as his.

Now, in the mortal
stillness of this house,
I sort his notebooks,
breathe the scent
of tobacco pellets pressed
between brown photographs;
pocket a pencil stub;
his desk, lost in my shadow.

Michael Croshaw

The Other Side of the Story

We talked of trivial topics,
touched on agriculture and seasons' passing,
roughness of country tracks and surly ways
of rural folk who, sullen, unsociable,
greet strangers with invincible distrust.
I told him of a horse I'd bought that week,
and so we reached my errand.   Business matters
absorbed us for an hour, then I left.

But mainly I recall, these many years,
constant distraction of his wayward eyes,
that moved from me, instinct with far-off glaze,
as if, through hallway, door and fowl-stalked yard,
they fathomed distant perspectives, waterfalls
in a remote and radiant country shining,
or framed a clash of arms beyond the hills.
Some demon of the spirit rode him, loosed –
as in dark dream – imagination's bonds,
and he was ice and flame in alternation.

Mere fancy?   No, for rid of me at last
I know he chased a vision to its end,
beyond the thrones of summer to the wells
where silence mouths in long slow drops its cool
and channelled murmur to absorbing cells.

From some gold city of the sun I'd kept
a poet too long, constraining him to lose
the epic thread that, ordering him from sleep,
but for my advent might indeed have torn
lost mystery from the thorn that guards the rose,
in furious webs of fire discerned dead kings
whose voices, thundering till his brain would burst,
had yielded him their secret while he slept.

Mervyn Linford
Talking To The Bees

What to do when a friend goes mad –
When the head lets loose its fragments like a swarm
And every sting is barbed to pump its venom.
When the wings of words fan at the hive's lip
And dance the dance of convolute direction.
What comb within the darkness that surrounds
Will ever drip the sweetness it deserves
When every cell is shrouded under wax.
I am no keeper of the bees –
I turn afraid from urges that react –
That leave the air cacophonous with anger.
Behind the veil I watch the flameless smoke;
And though I talk, the bees are still disturbed
Will not accept the mask of my composure.

Evangeline Patterson

Lucifer at the Fair

Blowing my last bob
on the Jungle Ride, I saw him.
Tawny and lithe as a hunting
cat, he balanced and swayed
on the racketing heave of the boards.
I whirled like an atom around him

to thunderous music.
He took my shilling, gazing aloof,
while I, thin as a lizard,
with skinned knees, went bucketing
past, uncoveted prize in my
striped school dress.   If he'd spoken
a word to me, I'd have died.

For hours I lay, seeing,
printed on night, him
glow like a dark angel
at the heart of his whirring planet.

Brian Louis Pearce

Oxford Movement

Trees, I salute you, red,
yellow, dun, in your down-
turning.
Autumn's brought you to bed
in a study of brown
yearning.

Sunset one moment, next
soft green solace takes you,
learning
how joy breaks from its text,
blends, flies to you, shakes you,
burning.

Leaves at their leaving are
like men most vividly
discerning
their pageant's fixed Christ-star
blacked out, then lividly
returning.

Thought, aspiration, die
or seem to, after flowering,
urning;
yet kick, glow, blow the sky
of feeling high, endowering
learning.

Lachlan Mackinnon

Blooms

I

There is a dead frog on the lawn, glistening,
untouchable.   At first we think the cat, our
guardsmanlike water-bailiff, and indeed
he will have fished it out, but this creature
has been flattened by some disaster.
Deduction travels slowly backwards
like Theseus to our infant daughter
plonking brick-ends into the splashy pond.
The frog must have risen as we hope our souls might
through the mucky layers to open light.

II

The shrub stoops to us, but is still taller
than the kitchen door plus the steps.   The more it sheds
of its pink bell-shaped flowers, sized and flared
like the candleholders on a child's birthday cake,
the more it blooms, seemingly inexhaustible.
This would be a child some centuries old.
No perfectionist, it excels itself
daily, each morning brighter than the last.

Kathleen Raine
Honesty

Too long astray –
Time, from hour to hour,
Lifelong, unending departure –

In my withering garden
A country flower,
'Honesty', prized for its signature,

Because, its seeds set,
Fall from a clear membrane,
Emblem of pure intent.

I thought to have come indoors
Not to this room
But to another, as it was,

Honesty and dried grass
In an alabaster vase,
Lamp alight, curtains drawn,
Against the night –

Childhood, the holy day –
A moment, a turning away,
And never again.

Peter Dale

A Woman Speaks to our Father

Lord of the entire universe,
was there no one else to take?
No lively son in the womb's hearse,
no supple girl for you to break?

But you must take my dolphin man?
No boy to fall to you in play,
no white head broken like a fan,
no sinewed arm for you to fray?

Must I be jealous all my life
of six foot of claggy earth;
jealous of every trotting wife,
of every brat that's given birth?

I am jealous of you, God.
If I had every inch your might,
in my black hole you'd spoil your rod;
you'd kick up stars in endless night.

Ian Parks

Night Thoughts

The sea under my window
all night long repeats its theme
like some momentous hymn:
wave upon wave its rhythms come,

rising and falling through the hours
of sleep. This night takes
from us that which is not ours:

our warm breath turned to dew on the cold pane.
Like some momentous hymn,
though wordlessly, the sound the sea makes

has in it the stifled echo of a dream.
Rising and falling through the hours
of sleep, your steady breathing overlays

the soft roar of the sea; repeats its theme
with wordless rhythms of its own. Our days
have in their constant ebb and flow
the stifled echo of a dream.

Graham Mort
Flowering Currant

Sunlight torrents through thin glass,
Glares upon the rhythmical breathing
Of the classroom.
Hands are a study of pen-grips, faces
A stucco of bewilderment, screwed up
Against interrogative light.

Examination papers whisper, leaf
After leaf shivers in the faint
Draught their breathing makes.

Sun fires a spray of flowering currant
On the teacher's desk, water magnifies
Torn stems, bubbles cling, their eggs
Hatching silver embryos.

Sullen faces look up through shafts
Of almost invisible dust;
They peer through its faint hologram
At the intolerable hieroglyphics of knowledge.

The teacher looks out at an emerald rugby pitch
Where tall white gallows rise at either end;
Bleached figures wave on the cricket square
Towards a lost ball flown over gully.

He fingers the flowers' red droplets as
Light finds copper in the children's hair,
Amazed at how his feelings still melt to theirs;
He wonders where the time ebbed, at how
He held and spilled moment after moment
From the liquid of his life.

William Oxley
Horses in Winter

Alone or in pairs like penitents they stand
in unholy wind at the bleakest edge
of fields of winter-gutted farmland
where inedible ivy clings to crazy walls
and trees offer bare ideas of form and age.
Some wear coats like men in shabby overalls
or chamois-naked stand log-still
fetlocked in a mash of ice and mud.
I marvel at their patience in such chill,
spare-ribbed statues of neglect whose
wincing flanks betray frost-detected blood,
and think they have a dream
of long stalked days of green to come:
a special dream – they must! – that will preserve
a sanity and hope in horsey gloom
which nature files for all who do deserve
some help through days of pre-death death
when wind would drill the stars from night
and freeze to glass bouquets a horse's breath
vainly cropping at rigid spikes of spite
and withered fodder far withdrawn
in nettled corners of each sunless dawn.

P.J.Kavanagh
VE Day

'We'll follow the man with the big cigar'
Unembarrassed they sing on the VE tape of ITMA,
Clarrie, Sid, Jack Train, little Jean Capra,
All the classless troupers of my childhood,
Concert-party soubrettes, tenors from ends of piers,
Brought together by Tommy and my father.

Some of the jokes will do, but others strain
Too much – 'I went home by Underground.
Fell down a manhole and caught the last drain' –
Its awfulness almost pricking filial tears
Because of a lost, genial metre in there,
Unpretentious dactylics, a signalling thump at the end

Which the audience knew on its pulse.
Maybe not good Immortal work, not art.
But we'll not hear, however hard we try, the noise he
                                                    heard,
Withdrawn, unjaunty man, the generous sound
His genial rhythms provoked: frank gratitude,
An audience that stands and cheers, and cheers.

Hilary Davies
The Blind Man

He fumbles his way in, gazing at stars,
He has to rub eyes to restore composure.
Fragments of liquid, food, scatter his waistcoat and shirt,
His white banner he prefers to keep in his pocket furled:
He is clearly very discontent with all this.
Like a mountain he sits between us,
Big-bellied, uncaring, loud-voiced
Among the shadowy persons who erupt
Into his hand, demanding attention
And towards whom he cocks an ear
After they are long gone.   When the taxi
Swallows him, he settles thankfully
Into the humming of wheels,
Stares with his white sight
At all the candles of London.

Berenice Moore
The Screaming

The screaming woke me up again last night
I started out of sleep
screams trapped inside my head.
I wept as I remembered you.

Two years ahead of me at school
I hero-worshipped
Head Girl, Hockey Captain,
long blonde hair.

I tried to be the same –
an independent mind,
odd jobs and freedom,
jazz sessions in your flat,
talks after midnight,
sleeping on your floor.
One day I walked out of my father's home
to live my own life,
found that it was fun.

They called us drop-outs,
said we were no good.

That year we went round the Festivals,
to Glastonbury for Midsummer.
We washed our feet in the Holy well
and stood high on the Tor
to see the sun rise.

The slow drag up the long hill out of Bath
with engine over-heating crawled along.
The lorry screamed towards us, seemed
as if it hurtled through the air.
I saw the driver's face quite blank,

pallid with staring eyes and open mouth.
I heard his soundless shouts
before the crash, almighty bang, crunch
breaking glass, the hiss of steam
and dreadful sudden quiet.

They let me see you once,
all white, all bottles, tubes and wires.
Your eyes were shut.
I watched the blue light
waver up and down.

That was the last summer of my innocence.

Anna Adams
A Portrait

She takes a pride in ordinariness;
    a consciousness of gifts, or seething brain
have never driven her to evening class;
    her schooling was completed at fourteen.
One might say that her small-browed cranium,
    wrinkled with puzzlement, scarcely demanded
    frontal lobotomy to make contented
with housework, knitting and geranium,
her unambitious soul.   She shuns disgrace
    and pays her rent and spins her money out,
and cleans and decorates her dwelling place,
    unhampered by excessive thought or doubt.

But this is far from ordinariness:
    she also lacks resentment, which is rare;
though cosmic angst is for the student-class,
    non-intellectuals can achieve despair.
Although her wisdom is expressed in proverbs:
    least said is soonest mended – never mind –
    a stitch in time – it's an ill wind – I've found
an unpretentious guru of the suburbs.
Transplanted now, and rooted in the north,
    her virtues are quite real. Lack of wit
is not a guarantee of moral worth;
    she also lacks greed, bigotry and spite.

Contentment is not ordinariness,
    and loving-kindness is not common either;
nor is imagination – the reverse –
    she knows that unseen refuge from dull weather.
Inhabitants of authors' printed pages
    accompany her afternoons. They move

before her inner eye; she feels real love
for shadow-puppets on fictitious stages.
She goes time-travelling inside her head
        through Chekhov's Russia or Tom Hardy's Dorset,
with ineffectual, misunderstood
        heroes that touch the heart beneath her corset.

Her commonplace extraordinariness
        infects her housework. This is no mere chore
but art, which makes her unzip and undress
        and dress in different colours each armchair.
She searches for the perfect composition
        and perfect colour scheme; her media
        are curtains, carpets, gimcrack furniture,
all undergoing constant transformation
which changes nothing. 'Passes time away,'
        she says, as though time needed help to fly:
'It keeps me occupied.' Her energy
        remains unbaffled by the question Why.

And all this ordinary busyness
        contains the mystery of difference;
her ways of doing what her neighbour does
        are different. Unique. Her common-sense
is mutant. She pays death-insurance pence
        and calls it saving up for her old age,
        smiling as calmly as a Buddhist sage.
Her theological indifference,
myopic interest in what's at hand –
        her scrap of garden and the market place –
confer a grace, for, to her trustful mind,
        brief days, not grand eternity, suffice.

John Gurney
The Acacia Tree, St. Edmund Hall, Oxford

St. Edmund Hall is quieter than it was
in the old days.
More clerical.
The laughter of the drinking-men has gone
from the green lawn.
The silence hangs like mist.   Is palpable
and scholarly.
One notices the beauty of the tree.

I watch it as a bell begins to chime.
It charms my ear
as rapidly
the now that flows away is making time
and the next night.
The leaves of the acacia seem to be
translucent, sere,
as golden as the lanes of Oxfordshire.

The students move along from thought to thought
more anxiously
than I before
would draw my worn awareness, twist, distort
whatever caught
my fancy's dream: would ponder, half-explore
how God could be
the author of his own eternity.

But now the tree is aging, and its fall
is probable.
Propped up, it slumps
its thick trunk at the warm south-facing wall,
the beautiful
wisteria and the sundial and the pump

and the wide well.
It seems the bell is tolling out its knell.

Life's syllable is swift. And yet the leaves' delight
knows no abyss:
illuminates
the tall New College trees' sublimer height
with quiet light
as if deep roots had pierced, still penetrate
their base of bliss,
the golden understanding of what Is.

Kathleen Raine

Dream

I am become a stranger to my dreams,
Their places unknown. A bridge there was
Over the lovely waters of the Tyne, my mother
Was with me, we were almost there,
It seemed, but in that almost opened valley
Extending and expanding, wind-sculptured sand;
Dry its paths, a beautiful waterless waste
Without one green leaf, sand-coloured behind closed eyes.
That film shifts, but the arid place remains
When day returns. Yet we were still going towards the Tyne,
That green riverside where childhood's flowers
Were growing still, my mother and I, she dead
With me forever in that dream.

Vernon Scannell

Flying Blind

Soft, blundering fog has neutralized
The morning sky, and from that foul
And padded air is recognised
The aircraft's stretched catarrhal growl.

A plane about to land, we hope
In safety though, on looking through
Imagination's telescope,
We see that they are hoping too.

And some within that metal case
Dictate a message straight to God;
They stare through glass but only face
The day's enormous smothering wad.

It bandages the windows tight
However much they crane and peer;
Their voices flutter on a bright
Chatty thread of perfect fear.

Everyone becomes a blind
Longing for the feel of earth
Beneath his feet, amazed to find
How much one stepping-stone is worth.

And they are right to be afraid,
But wrong to fear the aircraft's fate,
For they should fear the ambuscade,
Those terrorists beyond the gate.

Duncan Forbes
Moggie Thatcher

My name is Moggie Thatcher, I'm a biter and a scratcher,
    I'm renowned for landing on my feline feet.
I'm the grocer's puss from Grantham, who became the National
                                  Anthem
    And I like expensive cuts of public meat.
Though painted as the brashest tyrannical old Fascist
    To rule the land without the common touch,
I'm proud to think I'm British and both resolute and skittish –
    You don't kick Iron Lady in the crutch.

My name is Moggie Thatcher, I'm a biter and a scratcher,
    And survival is the nature of the beast,
Working late and with the light on, at the Grand Hotel in
                                 Brighton,
    I've got another seven lives at least.
My culture is the gin-set, the Finchley pearls and twinset,
    Britannia reincarnate rules the waves!
Britannia reincarnate in the streets of Friern Barnet,
    The unemployed can be employed as slaves.

R.S. Thomas

Match My Moments

That time
the soldiers broke in
to my room and I,
the sword at my throat,
looked up from my sums
and theorems and smiling
said: 'Spare my designs.'

That time
in the rustling bracken
the road ran with sheep,
a woollen river but vocal,
saying in its raw baritone
to the man on its banks:
'We give our life for the shepherd.'

That time
the queue winding towards
the gas chambers and the nun,
who had already died
to this world, to the girl
in tears: 'Don't cry. Look,
I will take your place.'

That time
after the night's frost the tree
weeping, the miser in me
complaining: 'Why all this washing
the earth's feet in gold?'
and I, my finger at my lips: 'Because
it is what we are made of.'

Peter Abbs

At the Extremities

This evening, under tumultuous cloud, stubble
Burns, cracks and smoulders; the fields are stark
Rectangles of death; flints glint from rubble
And furrow; outstrips of chalk gash the dark.
I imagine Persephone drifting here,
Singed poppies limp in her scarlet dress,
Her drugged mind, disconsolate, driven near
The sudden gap in things where Hades is.

I think of Tolstoy, restless, to the end
Passionate for horizons, tracked by cameramen;
At the last station of his half-cracked mind
Whispering: *I must go on. I must go on.*
And now a crescent moon drifts over the Downs –
Brief glimmering sign above flint boundaries.

Anne Ashworth

A Far Country

I have been to a far country.
How can I make report?
I do not know its name.
Ignorance shames me.

They question me with eyes.
How do you feel? they say.
But they mean,
                    What was it like?
        That far country –
        do you bring good news from there?
        Do they have laws or is there anarchy?
        How do you travel?
I answer them with eyes.

I feel quite well, I say.
But I mean,
                    How can I tell you?
        That far country –
        Its colours are not in our palette.
        The grass is on fire with love
        till mountains shimmer in smoke
        but a bush is not consumed.
        Savage, its breakers dash you against rocks
        but without a sound,
        and this is the sea's love dance.
        Words are torn and burnt
        in a consuming Yes.

        Laws?   There are no laws
        but it is not anarchy,
        that torrent's rage, that still pool of love,
        and all the news is good.

You have to travel on silence.
I know no package tours,
can offer you no tickets.
They are not transferable.
If there are regulations for passengers
I have no copies.

I answer them with eyes:
I look at them with love.
But then I fear to scorch them
and draw a curtain quickly across my face
and pretend I am not well
and again I am ashamed.

Ashamed of ignorance: what do I have to tell?
Ashamed of silence: where have my words gone?
Ashamed of curtains: why do I crouch and hide?

How can I say, he is burning my words away?
How can I say, his love is a fire of silence?
How can I say, I do not know his name?

Rosamund Stanhope
A Visitation

Packed against the cold
with the fire of Genesis, the gospel's
sirocco, hoping perhaps
for fruit cake and tea
or at least a kindly chat
about Armageddon, God's covenant
and the possibility of snow at Christmas
they smile from the threshold, Bible in hand
evangelical musket primed

just when you're about to write an imperishable
epode, or prepare the
duck Maréchale with *sauce poivrade*
or four minutes into your call to
Beverley Massachusetts;   happy in their
assurance of reception, the new cashmere coat
the certainty of righteousness
chapter twenty-one of Revelation
and the hundred and thirteenth psalm.

Rebuffed, they rebound
from the shutting door, feeling a little
foolish, maybe, identifying
with the Son of Man, who, likewise, had
nowhere to lay his head;
but aware that you are so much the poorer
for not being regenerated by
'I would not have you ignorant, brethren ...'
'And the Lord accepted Job';

never suspecting that you, who
deplore happy endings
seeing them scurry down the path
shoulders a trifle bowed
nonetheless straggle back to
the trite verse, the murdered bird
the waste of money and time on a call to the States,
conscious that the gilt has left the
sultana almond twist;   that you have
indeed experienced
a visitation.

Robert Greacen
Bad Books

Bad books could raise the devil –
A man he knew had done just that
And later hanged himself.
The story came from Uncle George
Who, neighbours said, had never lied.
Impressed, I vowed to spurn bad books,
To sip the master spirits' blood,
Read all Shakespeare by twenty-one,
In time grow wise, armoured in light.
Yet bad books sidled onto my shelves –
Lightweight novels, shallow philosophy
That dared to join the Great and Good.
The trick, perhaps, is knowing which is which.

Harry Guest
A Daughter's First Term at University

You've said good-bye. She's standing in the car park.
You know there are mallards on that pool in the quadrangle.
A Virginia Creeper sprawls crimson by her balcony.
Later a heron will visit those fields beyond suburbs
but now she has no map to decipher tomorrow,
the clock-face is unyielding, the brochure's out of date, she must
invent a city from scratch and fix names on to strangers.
You know all this. The windscreen-wiper doesn't clear your tears.

'Phone-calls with costs reversed will assure you that certain
seminars are fun, friends have been found. The fact remains –
the one whom you loved as an everyday presence has been
elected citizen of a world you'll never inhabit.
She's left, rightly so, to gain where others have given,
she's cut the cord, packed her bags, embarked on adulthood,
leaving a shadowy stair-well humming with memories
up which you'll clamber trying to tune in to the past.

When she returns, the week-day thrown open in welcome
will lead again to the stunted monolith, the marsh with its orchids.
From time to time you'll stand together on the same
light bridge, high-arched, under which the long-legged
ibises strut with ludicrous, delicate care.
You'll watch with pride the way her hands brush dirt off strange
and gleaming ores. You'll be given fragmentary
and garbled accounts of patterns made, unwoven,
forged again in distant centuries and ivory rooms.
You'll pay attention but she's gone so far you'll never quite
catch up that unfamiliar figure on the changing fields.

Colin H.E. Wiltshire
Paolo and Francesca

The wind has torn them both away
From every concept they have known.
The wind is now the earth to them,
And meat and drink and breath to them.
The sky they flounder in is grey.
The wind chills and entombs like stone.

This is not hell, and cannot be
While my Paolo is here with me.

Each dead, locked in the other's clasp,
(His head, his lips are on her breast),
They cannot ever now be free
From their fatal unchastity.
What heaven is they cannot grasp,
Condemned to think their love the best.

This is not hell and cannot be
Francesca is still here with me.

But rumours God cannot suppress
That they are happy in their dream,
Love's heroes who show no remorse,
Arise on earth and spread. Of course
What their love is God may not guess.
True love is love of what's supreme.

This is not hell, they say, and cannot be
With the beloved here with me.

53

J.P. Ward
Lights in the Fog

Visibility yards.
Villagers long indoors.

Off the Atlantic it settles
On the gorse-and-bracken hill.

Round hinges of gates and tufts
Rolls its war-zone barbed wire.

Lights in the paring fog
Loom down, each woolled

By a halo suspended
Between gravity and mystery

While wisps filter up from
Wet tarmac as if a deep

Underworld were now smoking.
Unseen good demons met below.

Heaving like a ferry, our sole
Hotel's decks carry bulbs

Strung out for Xmas joys.
'Saxon Inn' on its bows.

D.J.Enright
Wonders Of Nature

In preparation for the dry season
Certain creatures
Store water in their bodies
Burrow into the sand
Grow a heat-repelling lacquer
On their skin –
And sleep it out.
The dry season
Alternates with the wet season.
When the wet season begins
The creatures come to life
Emerging from the sand
Casting off the lacquer
Slim and fit
Sharp and hungry
How they come to life! –
The wet season lasts about a week.

David Sutton

At the Funeral

Funerals of the old are for the old:
The young, even the middle-aged, intrude,
Stiff in their unpractised piety,
Distracted by oak poppyheads, by light
From stained glass windows blue as irises.
There may be grief, but they are grateful too
To simplifying death that has unpicked
This knot of care from their much-tangled lives.
It is the old that mourn without alloy,
That shoulder loss and lay it to its rest.

Who are they though, so lusty at the back
With lifted voice, needing no book of hymns,
The sad spruce women and the grey-haired men?
What is it that they stare at past the air?
Outside, in winter sunlight, all's revealed:
The cousins of her youth, friends, neighbours, come
To honour old acquaintanceship; now lives
Like long-divided rivers meet again,
A swirling confluence of memory
Carries the dead one to the final sea.

How gently they exclude one. "That would be
Before your time." "That's going back a bit."
But always to such time they do go back:
To rationing, the Blitz, heroic toil,
The fields of childhood, legendary snows,
Shops, terraces long gone. I understand:
Each dying nerves a new resistance, firms
A final bond of shared exclusiveness.
This is a closing ranks: like pioneers
They man the dwindling circle of their days.

The January sunlight has turned cold.
The ceremony's over. They depart
Down unsafe streets to doors they must keep locked.
What they came to do is done: somewhere
A girl they knew is running over grass
In a green country, leaving them behind
To counters and containments, ritual
And stoic unsurprise, such as they use
Whose lives have fed on long adversity,
Who know betrayal, and will not betray.

Robert Nye

Riposte

Above all other nights that night be blessed
On which my grandam rose from her sweet rest
Woke by a nightingale whose passionate song
Rang in the moonlight, Keatsian and long.
My grandmother threw open wide her door
And listened for a minute, not much more;
Then, when sufficient nightingale she'd heard,
Cried out: *Right! Just you bugger off, you bird!*

Gavin Ewart

The Generations

We always think we can do better.
The atheist father and the Catholic convent daughter.

But it's never the same; it's not rhyming but assonance;
it's not exactly an echo – though there is resonance,

a kind of ghost of an unscanned similarity.
Apples don't fall far from trees. And if we take Verity

as the type of all left-hand spin bowlers, there's a family
                                                    resemblance,
greatest or least. Don't ring for an ambulance

or have a heart attack if a son turns totalitarian –
or turns his back on politics – or studies Ancient Sumerian

cryptography. Evolution demands variation.
And to be Not-The-Same is a permanent teenage ambition.

So they are like us or not. Just as we are, perhaps, like our fathers.
In the end too perhaps (you could say) nobody bothers.

We haven't improved things much. There are still wars and murders
and armaments and big corporations, capital punishment, prisons
                                                    and warders.

Of course, we could call it a day and blow ourselves up.
The Big Bang. Or a whimper, as Ecology brings us all to a stop.

Adam Johnson
December 1989

The nascent winter turns
Each root into a nail,
And in the West there burns
A sun morbid and pale.

Now, from the city bars
We drift, into a cool
Gymnasium of stars –
The drunkard and the fool:

Into the night we go,
Finding our separate ways –
The darkness fraught with snow,
The leaves falling like days.

Alan Hester
An Essay on the Twentieth Century

Apparently they knew exactly what they were doing.
They had the information, but as long as they could
They denied it was happening. They watched,
As one by one the lives went out.
First, the ones they couldn't miss:
Whales, elephants, the Great Cats.
Then, the ones they didn't consider as living,
And all the links that one by one
Went missing, as they exercised their right
To multiply, to hold dominion
Over the earth, and the sea, and the beasts.

In the West of Europe, (Pay attention, boy!)
There was a period of some two hundred years
From, probably, the eighteenth century,
To early in the twenty-first, when circumstances
Caused a limited experiment in political systems.
Who can remember what this was called?
Well done, "Democracy." This was the name for
Government by popular consent and participation,
And was made possible by the coincidence
Of an abundance of natural resources.

These resources were put to use with great skill
And huge machines were made, and people travelled.
There are records of travel by land, air and sea.
One day they say we'll rediscover those things.
Boys and girls, I hope to hell we don't.

The people elected those who put themselves forward
For election, and compounded this by imagining
This meant they no longer had to think themselves.
They used what they were given

And they needed things they'd never thought about.
Tonight, I'd like an essay on the twentieth century.
You can use the drawings to help you.
Imagine you're a person living then.
Try to understand them.
You know the answer's in your hand

Derek Stanford
Poem for a Late Autumn Birthday

The mason bee, before it hibernates
(this crumbling flower-set wall its winter home),
busies itself in pollen-gathering,
each shortening day a late yet sweet addition
to that long hoarding all its life has known.

Yes, I am stirred, hearing such lively music
active between whiles in this quietening place.
More cheerfully I view the haloed sun,
though intermittent falls its lengthening beam.

The bee's last labouring redeems the time,
and every idle leaf's a thought suspended.

Mount Pleasant, Reigate, October 1989.

Carole Satyamurti
In-Patient

I have inherited another woman's flowers.
She's left no after-scent, fallen hairs,
no echoes of her voice,
no sign of who or how she was

or through which door she made her exit.
Only these bouquets – carnations,
tiger lilies, freesias, hothouse roses,
meretricious everlasting flowers.

By day, they form the set in which I play
the patient – one of a long line
of actresses who've played the part
on this small white stage.

It's a script rich in alternatives.
Each reading reveals something new,
so I perform variously – not falsehoods,
just the interpretations I can manage.

At night, the flowers are oracles.
Sometimes they seem to promise a long run;
then frighten me with their bowing heads,
their hint of swan songs.

William Baer

A Fragile Beauty Never Seen

And then, one night, we brought ourselves together,
and, shocked, she spoke of shattering days of pain,
of cold, confused, and dark despairs like mine –
and long, pernicious, black and endless nights.
And so, without conviction, we spoke of parting,
certain, somehow, that neither would walk away –
and slowly, slowly, in that darkest night,
she finally, softly, fell back in my arms.

And we would spend that long and perfect
night, watching the stars forever, refinding our way –
and comprehending love, convinced again,
that we're among those few still doomed to last.
And then, near dawn, I held her close again,
as light new suns reflected in her face,
and touched her hair, and watched her close her eyes,
and held a fragile beauty – never seen.

Kathleen Raine

An Old Woman's Spell

(For three sad women)

What are words
That they can comfort
A woman's sorrow?
May my long ago
Bring healing now
To present pain
In words from the heart
That love has spoken
Over and over,
Mother to son
And mother to daughter,
To the new-born, the dying,
By the lonely to God,
To no-one, to the stars,
To the night, to the cat,
To the absent, to the embers,
Love's words spoken
By the dead to the unborn,
Too late, too soon,
To the once, to the gone,
Helpless and comfortless
Love speaks a language
Simple as silence.
How many weepers
Have bathed our eyes
In those cold waters
That rise from the deeps
Whence all tears flow?

***

From words I have spun
My nettle-yarn,
Spells of healing
To clothe the sorrowers,
The generations
Who in turn must weave
The veils of love,
Shawls for the babes
And shrouds for the dying.

***

The turquoise summer evening sky
Asked, 'Why stay below, for here
Spaces are infinite where angels are
Unbounded from star to star.'

I replied, 'Soul builds her house
In the fleeting here and now
Of once and never again for ever –
What do angels know
Of the human ways of sorrow?'

Sky said, 'You will be returning
Soon to where memory gives place
To ever-presence,' and I
'Through lifelong years we love
Dear human faces that must die.'

Phil Madden

Treat Me Gently Today

Treat me gently today
milkman, shopkeeper,
stranger with whom I exchange.
The girl from next door is getting married.
She was born the same year as Rebecca.

We are always reminded
at the turn of life's seasons
of all that she will never be.

The different bus to the different school,
the calling of names not the calling to play.
When the others went out to the party
she put lipstick all over her dolls,
and there is no beauty
that could make up for that.
And I've often wanted to give her away
be free for my journey to the rest of my age.

And I always wanted to give her away
set sail on her journey
with a tear and champagne.
The bells are ringing.
They take their toll.
So treat me gently today
milkman, shopkeeper,
stranger with whom I exchange.

Adam Johnson
View from the Monument

Take the three hundred and eleven stairs
(There is no lift), observing as you climb
The nature of the spiral – that it dares
Contest the uniformity of time –

Such eccentricities are why we came:
Wren's Monument – a city's ancient grief
That smoulders in a copper vase of flame,
And Cibber's allegorical relief.

An urban panorama now affords
The true perspective of a vicious age.
The streets we name are nothing more than words
That read in valediction from the page:

Old Jewry, Savage Gardens, Pudding Lane –
Enduring in the wake of enterprise
They cower in the shadow of the crane.
In ranks like weeds the gleaming towers rise:

Encroaching on our vision, they abuse
More than the level aspect of the sky.
Each, from below, the grasping magnate views –
Theirs are our cities, though the cities die.

C. H. Sisson
Steps to the Temple

What is belief? A recognition?
Who knows of what? If any say
He knows, he lies.
Who knows what never was begun
And will not end? God is a way,
And a surprise.

And in that way we cannot choose,
For choice deceives us, as it must.
We live in sense, certain at least that we shall lose
That urgency, for we are dust.
Our recompense,

If any, cannot be to find
That beauty and that bitterness
Again. A new
Perception must await the vanished mind:
Or none, and which of these we cannot guess.
That much is true.
So here, we who are fallible
As shifting sands, may feel the tide
Flow over us, or in, or out.
If in, then all will there be well;
If not, then we should feel no pride
Even in doubt.

Helen Farish
Saint Hilda's Churchyard

Wild garlic and pink hawthorn,
Bluebells and grass the height of hay.
My love, at Saint Hilda's churchyard
I imagined your light bones
Under the weight of flowers,
Their roots prevented you from seeing
Which season ruled your plot.

We will spend our lives together
And I will wear a wreath of stone
When I am left here without you.
If only I believed we could dance eternally
On the floor of our memories,
That the final partings will last
No longer than the bluebells.

Grass grows the height of hay
At Saint Hilda's churchyard
And 'Together Again' are the only words
To reach above.

Julian May

The Telling

*Some Islamic men will never again touch a daughter once
she reaches puberty.*

This life, so close we knew
before the telling – now, it's over.
We all know that, your mother, you
and I.

I tell you, go, cover
those careless limbs. Above all hide
that fear, naked in your child's eyes.
Go veil it with a woman's pride,
the knowledge that this wound is wise
beyond all telling.
Stop. Don't run into my arms;
there is no comfort left,
only danger hidden in their warmth.

Soon, you will have my parting gift:
a choice husband to walk behind
those three paces of duty. A man as kind
as I am, a life so close you'll know
before the telling.

I tell you, this one is gone.
Though it seems too soon for you to go
I've lost you, to the tugging of this crescent moon.

Leah Fritz

Holiday in Les Halles

Here in the centre of the Paris circus
the whore and her dog go round and round their beat.
She stops to chat with the Chinese waitress
and other passing neighbours in the street.

The men walk by. Nobody takes her up.
A tight bra pinches her shoulder blades.
The dog's been collared since he was a pup.
They've both seen younger if not better days.

Neither remembers running free on grass.
They share one look: love me, make me real.
And all are like that in this cul-de-sac —
slim boys in jeans, girls in killing heels,
I bonded to this window, waiting for you
cruising other Paris avenues.

Fred Beake

Signs

The Romans to resolve
their death-grapple with Hannibal

sent a fair part of their cabinet
half the known world

to fetch a chancy god
from Asia Minor

When I was pruning
the Reverend Goodman's apple tree

nostalgic for a love
that shall not be repeated

an apple on a twig
brushed me with new beginnings

Somewhere beyond hopelessness
the two connect

Frederic Vanson
Not Quite Mendelssohn

The world resumes its ancient ways
As spring asserts in buds and sprays
The sun's new equinox.

The blackbird's busy in the hedge
There's song in woodland, field and sedge
And no wind rocks

The bough, the sky's one even blue
The myth of paradise seems true,
No chill wind mocks.

All's innocent as it began
Except the riven heart of man
That ancient paradox.

John Gurney

Clare at Lippett's Hill

But who was there to talk to? Who was there
to listen to his language sparingly
and talk about the badness in the air,
the black melt of the night? And how could trees
communicate, exhausted as they were
by fighting one another and the wind
that tangled up the forest, made a slur
of foliage? Something in the mind
must surely have been longing to confess
to someone non-judgemental, someone who
could listen to his fictions and undress
the wounds of his illusions, find a clue
to understanding Clare's fulminating oaths
at women, and their complex underclothes.

Sue Hubbard
Assimilation

I never knew whether to say Amen.
In the vaulted hall silent girls dipped
rosy profiles into dust freckled sunlight

while I stood dumb-lipped trapped by
the trinity of longing, fear, propriety,
the word still-born in my throat.

Alone at thirteen in shadows of Dresden
blue, I bore the guilt of history, somehow
felt the weight of censure for what 'they'd done'.

Head bowed consulting the diamond perforations on
regulation shoes, burnt ashes branded my tongue
with the double stigmata: unbeliever, hypocrite.

I did not know where I'd come from but guessed
at a journey through the snow flecked storms
of some Lithuanian December night

creeping through purple larch and spruce to flee
the zealous pogroms and their indignant Slavic rage.
Yet I've never tasted the sweet wine of Kiddush.

Beyond the stained glass windows and the Annunciation
English playing fields stretched printed with
tramlines, the watermark of fair play and impartiality.

In the back of the cupboard in my father's study
a tarnished silver samovar lay in waiting for
tall glasses, lemon and a scoop of Russian tea.

James Brockway

The Jackdaws

They cluster in the dying light, land in the firs,
then sweep the sky again, a shawl of birds
so dense, the air turns black.

One evening, a month before you died,
back they came, covered the rooftops
with their quivering, cut the sky with caws.

I took it for a sign. What your eyes saw
you did not say. You turned away,
sat down alone and lit a cigarette.

Tonight they are back again, they are swirling through
the gathering dark. I turn away,
sit down alone and light a cigarette.

Frances Wilson

The Danger of Gardens

Make no mistake, this is a sun trap.
Look where light reflected from the window's
glass bleaches the privet's darkness.
Undeflected, it blazes into your skull.
Can you remember what you were thinking
only a moment ago? Can't you see
that chalky azure flutter from flower
to flower is flaked off, blistered sky?

If you must enter, wedge the gate open;
avoid high walls, wisteria's papery grapes,
the hum of bees under pleached limes.
It is enchantment. You will be drowned
in the wind's hiss that this is paradise.
Quick, pick up the whiff of nicotine,
the geranium scent of Sundays, a hint
of fox beneath the maytree's avalanche.

Don't fall for the scarlet sheen
which leads to the poppy's purple heart.
It is war paint. This is a jungle.
See how it has thickened overnight.
Stay too long and it will close in,
fatten you up with colour, scent, heat,
till you forget the way you came, the world
outside. Grow sluggish, drugged. Oblivious.

Lotte Kramer
Cocoon

She says she can't remember anything
Of people, language, town. Not even school
Where we were classmates. Her smile is frail
And hides behind her husband's hypnotising

Quietness. 'A Suffolk man', he beams
And squares his tweedy frame against some
Unseen advocates who might still claim
An inch of her. She is content, it seems,

To lose her early childhood; he is near.
Protector or destroyer, it's his war.
He underwrites her willed amnesia,
Helps her to stifle terror, exile, fear.

She is cocooned, safe as an English wife
Never to split that shell and crawl through love.

Michael Henry
Pelion and Ossa

Remember when we stopped at pubs
and you ordered button mushrooms
soaked and bacon-ripe...
you divided up your portions
and saved the best till last
but those of us who finished first would say:
'Look at that play of light behind!'
and as you turned your head in trust
we stabbed our forks like bayonets ...

you never learned
you never could resist the light...
studenthood, motherhood, a part-time job
and bacon was sizzling in the pan
and then the unnatural pallor
like a light bulb left on during the day ...

I wish I could distract you now
when all your troubles heap
Ossa upon Pelion.

Penelope Shuttle
Wish

The sky gift-wraps the world
in blue,
with cloud-ribbons and tags
marked, Asia, America;
the world hangs
from a green branch
of some great decorated tree,
whose roots are set deep in living fire,
whose star-tipped crest
rises high and far and shining and forever

a dream,
a fondness,
a thing I would make true;
here, with you. And with you.

Brian Louis Pearce

La Belle Dame de Merci

Do I hear movement? It is my Muse stirring.
Do I hear laughter? It is her low tone
so delicately, discreetly re-occurring,

distinct in voice, in every Muse I've known.
No one could be distressed to hear her coming.
No one could feel that they were turned to stone

for she, like water in the kitchen running,
the fount at Hampton Court, is quite at home
with wife and husband, child and old man sunning,

though those she touches see the waters foam
with inspiration of the impetuous wind.
She does not bid her chosen rack and roam,

but wraps round with her love those she may bind.
She is our breath already, bathes our bone
in spirit of berries, bright-eye of my mind.

Norman Kreitman

Down There

How on earth do they manage
who understand nothing?

Love, for example. If any among them reaches
simple competence they name a church in his honour.
For most it is grabbing, being grabbed.
    Some cannot even spell it.

Or time. Usually they stand like a knife-edge
to the wind, splitting it to slipstreams of remorse,
expectation. In quieter moments they see only
    a trickle of dry sand.

Naive about space, they pretend that here
is different from there. They always adopt perspectives,
extol the partial view, subvert every landscape
    in the squint of their vanity.

They turn aside, embarrassed, at what they call
the big abstractions. They case their heads in bone,
complain to each other of poor vocabulary.
    As if the blind lacked only words!

How, understanding nothing, do they manage
    down there on earth?

Ruth Padel
Rosa Silvestris Russica

John by Grace of God Botanist Royal,
from the British expedition
against Russia, 1618,

brings back a Russian vest.
"*Stockens without heels.*" Snow-boots
to walk on snow without sinking.

Soldiers die of frostbite, heartache,
diarrhoea, plague. He collates
"*Things by me Observe'd*"

falling most in love
with Russian roses. "*Wondros sweet*".
All the deck back

he keeps alive a Briar of Muscovy,
the ambuscade's one prize.
How else should a scientist work

but join the politicians'
raids on other worlds?
Afterwards he labours

in his South London garden
on the names of roses,
little lights of the field.

Dannie Abse
Divorce Proceedings
(Harriet's)

Am I, this April an April Fool?
I'll not accept your handshake-offer:
'Friendship' – though what persists of love
lies chilled in the past, illusory,
like the far voyaging light of a star.

I'm not benign like Shelley's Harriet, no,
though pregnant as she was and as wretched.
I'll not saccharine a suicide-note.
'Dear one, God bless and watch over you,'
then grow hideous in the Serpentine.

Or be helpless like pill-taking Sylvia,
incandescent with desperation,
those oneiric poems like SOS's,
before full-stopping the riderless heart
with the head, eyes open, in the oven.

Yet once, like her, I hoped for a hundred-
piece orchestra, and Brahms and Mahler,
not a thin dance-tune on a comb;
a happy-ever-after golden crown,
not a dunce's paper hat, twee and tatty.

Don't you see? It's the corybantic poetry
of love's adult passion I long for still,
its wild rhyming and its cadences
– this the dismayed heart of it –
not the attenuated prose of friendship,

your mild pity. God rot your smiling teeth.
The pretty blossom's looted, betrayed,
the wind and the cold of it – April's
practical joke: the trees' confetti
wet and finished in the gutters.

David H.W. Grubb
The Old Circus Horses

After that forest of applause, the old circus horses
rode out into a dream of green, forgetting the clowns
splitting faces, exploding cars and people falling through
the sky, the iron roar of lions, the lugubrious definitions
of elephants, the monstrous man in the centre dressed in red.

Now each day arrives like a gay balloon, kite, a piece
of easy music thrown up to spin in the sun. Now the
possibility of trees, grass, to become animal again; the
death of instructions, the bait, the bombast of hoops.

The old circus horses, finding their pace, their minds,
begin to move into the scent of slow dawns and long
mornings. Everything has slowed down. From the field
they can sense ancient fires, the deep blaze of creation;
towards evening they smell again the ancient heat of the planet.

Sophie Hannah
Call Yourself a Poet

I called myself an architect.
Designed a huge sky-scraper.
How powerful it looked, erect
Upon my piece of paper.
Presto! The housing problem solved!
(I'd had no formal training.)
My pride and joy collapsed, dissolved,
The day it started raining.

I gave up architecture then
And called myself a vet.
My failure, time and time again,
To save a well-loved pet
Annoyed the RSPCA.
They went around campaigning
And I was forced to move away.
(I'd had no formal training.)

My next career was plumbing.
Easy enough, you'd think,
But I spent hours drumming
My fingers on the sink,
Scared to approach the toilet.
All blockages remained,
Which somehow seemed to spoil it.
(Perhaps I should have trained.)

I didn't dare to drive a van
So I became a poet.
I couldn't rhyme, make sense or scan
Yet no-one seemed to know it.

I knew that I had hit upon
My ultimate vocation
The day I met an Oxford don
Who praised my innovation.

Only last week I found myself
The subject of a lecture;
My book on some professor's shelf.
So who needs architecture;
Knowledge of water pipes? What fools
Dabble in surgery?
Oh, how restrictive! All those rules!
While verse, my friends, is free.

Phoebe Hesketh

Anti Jeu d'Esprit

on being eighty-three

Doors are shutting all around me;
One by one the lights go out;
Drops of water rushing seaward
Drip reluctant from the spout.
Days, like sand, run through the hour-glass.
Run away from hand and head,
Unheld as bubbles blown and vanished.
Days are egg-shells where I tread.

Alice Kavounas
The Lizard

Black tongue of land
languishing in the mouth of Coverack
lapped at by pre-dawn
small-fisted waves.

a lull in the birdsong –
that gap in nature's soundtrack

Dredged from bleary seas
a haul of Celtic gold
coins the day.
Hour after hour
the gods gamble away
their morning's plunder.
Its value alters hourly –
brash as base metal by noon.
Locals avoid its whitened eye
hanging above them like a buzzard
fixing on invisible prey.

*

The day's sovereign
burnished by wind and
thin as a hunter watch
slides idly down the far side
of my unconquered afternoon
scouring the vast, cloud-filled pocket of blue.

The printing of shadows resumes.
The sea's uneven surface
reveals another day's
spilled currency; false light

trickling over each watery ridge.
Waves conveying nothing
while fisherman trawl deep.

The sea drinks in
the last of the earth's light.
I watch a silver hammock
rise amidst these blackening trees.

To the west, the ancient coin
melts into that distant hedge.
It leaves a glow as scarlet as the berries
clinging to the common hawthorn whose branches
scratch at its disappearing face.

Slowly, another night breathes out
settling on my shoulders its sequinned shawl.

Julia Casterton
The Gift

Emptiness. Nothing waiting to be said.
Want, need nothing.
Is not this also fulness?

To wait without desire – for what?

Ranks of candles lit for winter,
starlings that swarm
as the light fails in the park,
swirl and swarm around the lake,
pulsing in the bare trees
like lit darkness

pulsing with song that is not song
as the light goes in the short days,
rushes and quickenings of music
without shape, shaped only by
the sudden knowing swarm of bodies,
a massive shifting shape in the coming night,
a blown flame
rearing yet guarded as the dark comes.

Sound of light,
tuneless lines and swarms of light
that pierce and form
the growing dark.

Lance Lee
The South Sussex Downs

Everywhere the ancestral mind –
field, windbreak, barrow, altar: on the crests
warriors and horses etched in chalk
refuse to go away, like bad dreams.
Everywhere the ancestral wind, blue and silver –
Mary's colours, the mother the pilgrims loved
who once traced this road through Alfriston,
then abandoned with the dreams in chalk.
Light wheels across the shore-hugging sea:
rain falls with a thousand years' despair
and the downs hood their heads with dark mists

and then the amazing thing
the land takes itself back from us

swallowing every human sign except
the drunken will-o-the-wisp villages
that stumble in their muddy troughs.
"Can you feel the brooding?" asks my friend,
yes! I want to say, but I can't shake the terror
gripping my throat and then, huge,
the exhilaration:

as though
I rise from a trance on the hill, set free
by the land's freedom, made fully human
only by passing through.

Jack Clemo
T.E. Lawrence

Just here, in this crabbed Dorset hut,
  Lawrence, you pierced an Arabian saga, heights
Of valour and endurance, but
  Never the sound hearth's comforts, bridal rights.

You loved red barren sand.
  Detested marriage and St Paul:
Even at your door I cannot understand
  Such a creature's world at all.

I thrive on Pauline toughness, grace at home
  In awkward signatures of bliss
When seven or more pillars of crusty wisdom
  Crash as a creed transforms a kiss.

There was, of course, the fact
  That your birth was illegitimate.
This must be said with tact:
  It was, in your day, unfortunate.

You screened the bruise of shame,
  Clutched at a harsh material sanctity
Of drilled machines, war flame
  And danger's dubious mystery.

Did hints of a broad transcendence
  Strike as your motor-cycle roared
To the fatal thud? Perhaps the essence
  Of our debt to you is stored

In the track of Homer, your Odyssey,
  The tremulous Greek hope
Set in a new candour. Still, this house is empty,
  Voiceless to me. I have no taste for a grope.

Caroline Price
Video Games

We only bought them in the first place as he is so bright;
we thought they'd give a stimulus his school can't quite supply –
No – I'm sorry – David doesn't want to play tonight –

We never for a moment dreamt he'd take to them in quite
this way – but then some boys are like that with anything they
try.
We only bought them in the first place as he is so bright.

He's no trouble in the morning – up as soon as it is light;
evenings we hardly see him – when tea's done, off he'll fly –
No – I'm sorry – David doesn't want to play tonight –

The teacher who makes out he falls asleep in class, pays slight
attention to her, shows no will to learn – she should drop by!
We only bought them in the first place as he is so bright.

I admit we hoped a little modern culture, you know, might
unite him with the other boys – he's always been so shy –
No – I'm sorry – David doesn't want to play tonight –

But every time we ask him, he insists he's quite all right;
and our David is no fool. After all, we can't deny
we only bought them in the first place as he is so bright –
No – I'm sorry – David doesn't want to play tonight –

Francis Warner

On Epsom Downs

Those who created me have turned to light –
Those they created have remained my friends –
And round this bed of earth, their tryst, unite
Their far-flung children while a word commends
Her body to his chalk, while winter sun
Flecks the damp hill where a new world's begun.

The vigil through long nights is now complete.
How friendly to my touch that wooden chair
Was, and how hostile metal, while heartbeat,
Pulse, breathing changed and faltered into air
Leaving exhausted limbs rest for release
Through holy death, her long life's masterpiece,

Into a beauty that can never fade,
Into a marriage meadow-rich, unseen,
Whose scent, like summer wallflowers, will pervade
Our dusty days, whose memory, bell-clean
And clear can prove that love transcends the spade.
You teach us how to face death unafraid.

Dannie Abse

Ghosting for Mayakovsky

(His suicide note)

I

It's long past One and you must be asleep.
The quiet night's astonished by all the stars.
Why wake you now with a telegram like thunder?

So many thoughts of mystery the night can bring.
So what? Our love boat's on the rocks. Its sails
wrenched from the mast. No use in adding up the cost,

we're quits; no need to weigh our hearts and hurts
upon the scales. 'No Life without you,' once I said,
and now the strokes of Two thud down like heads from blocks.

Our story's over, iconoclast. I'm lost. I'm through.
No need to wake you with a telegram like thunder.
Art's imperative will make these lines come true.

II

Once I drew the Queen of Hearts,
now I'm dealt another card. A club. A two.
Once forbidden love lit up like paper
then it charred.

Once with verse of lightning and half in song
I told a daisy and the world
you loved me, you love me not,
and how worthless life unfurled would be
without you – like a single shoe.
I'll not limp along.

I'm shot. I'm through.
Queen of Hearts, O Queen of Hearts,
the imperatives of Art insist,
the lies of Art come true.

95

James Harpur
Golden Fish

Summer clouds stuffed with lassitude
Drop shadow down on this grey world,
On this water bordered by a muddy marsh
That tars the stalks of drooping sedge,
Where not even the aquamarine filament
Of a dragonfly can seem to implement
Its task to thrill the air and spin
Blue, over skims of green pond-skin.

Then as a flame concealed in a grate
Suddenly streams up in a rush of heat,
From under lily pads a live brand shot,
A glowing ember, a fish burning deep carrot
That flowed through the gloom propelled
By the copper fins of its rippling tail.
And now another from the same red hot mould
Followed the first. The two, snaking round
The ins and outs of murky tunnels,
Blazed out the blood-orange of sun cells
That had for years impaled their neutral skins,
Now fully charged to emanate, illumine
A trail through their Tartarean world.

In orbit round the outer edge they would
Vanish into darkness. But then like comets
Would return spurting back a track of flame,
Igniting the gluey depths of waterspace:
Would return as gods, golden, luminous,
Spreading glory through the surrounding mire,
Incarnated in bodies of frozen fire.

Shanta Acharya
After Great Struggle

After great struggle
descends
an alternative calm –

the mind's swirling sky
now emptied of its thoughts in snowstorm.

Wrapped up like trappist monks
the trees preserve an immaculate silence.

The cold wind shakes
this proud stillness

Into crumbling flakes,
mercilessly
smiling at the helpless struggle

To keep up appearances at all costs.

Strange faces
sheathed
move in these streets

Wanting a more direct relation with the sun.

John Cotton
Quiet
Franche-Comte, France

Once there was quiet in the valley,
We could hear the slow thoughts of mountains,
The breathing of small hills
And at evening the dark forest trees listening to the silence.

Then came traffic
And it was never the same.
The earth stopped hearing
And the still small voices were drowned.
Though sometimes in the small hours
The quiet will pay its sly secret visits
From where it waits ...

Wanda Barford:
About Silence

This morning I woke
to a new kind of silence –

not the silence
out of which music is made,

nor yet the silence
that precedes language,

or is like the chasm
between waves of the sea –

but an absolute silence
that engenders only itself,

as it might envelop
the windless moon

or deepen
the blackness of space ...

a silence
of which I was born

and to which I shall add
my own silent note

William Baer

The Artist of Fashion

Up, then down, the boulevard,
he led the bloody avant-garde,
and shocked the bores who bought his 'spit'
and revelled in its counterfeit.–
And everything he did was news:
he'd hurt the girls and beat the muse,
then conjure from some current ditch,
and play the game till he got rich.

And each and every academian
fell before this chic bohemian
And Paris found him *hors concours*
and begged for more and more and more ...
But now, late nights, when death comes near,
he'll think of Giotto and Vermeer,
of Titian, and those truly great,
and, in the dark, asphyxiate.

Wendy Bardsley
Foetus

What mystery lurks within those silent cells
dividing with indifferent certainty.
What spirit waits until the vessel is prepared,
then brings the heavy thud of soul
to rack the nerves upon the steely edge of Time.

You do not know yet how the bluebell,
thin as your new skin will be, reflects the sky,
how birds within still woods try choruses at dawn
and wonder at their brazened heraldry.

And I shall tell you how when that dawn breaks
the silver snake creeps over roofs of houses,
how the spider spins a lacy galaxy,
and with the sun cascades a jewelled morning.

Now you kick.
I feel your quickening,
feel the flush of blood across my face.

Is this the moment when all memory goes,
when the voices of the gods come fast
to split the waters with farewells,
and you set tight your quivering lip,
forget, and stiffen up your back,
to come to me?

Heather Buck

Village Builder and Undertaker

He quietly stood while we explained our plans
for alteration, change. On that same spot
some twenty years before his men closed in
this wall, bricked up the door,

which we are opening now, in hope that life
will take a sudden turn, stream in
as generous windows gather in the sun,
forgetting that no change of scene
will wake us from the coma of our living.

Daily he measures all the lengths between
our lives' expansions and contractions,
knowing that at the end our territory
will be confined to one small plot.
Who knows what doors we'll open then or close?
No artisan's skilled use of tool or screw
can keep the Absolute from that sealed box.

Julie Whitby
A Cavatina of Rain

Somewhere between
the night and grey-edged morning,
I lost a poem.
Since memory played false,
a few lines only remain,
the best of them:
a cavatina of rain.

So slight a loss,
how painless this must have been
appears on remembering –
somewhere between
the night and grey-edged morning –
irreplaceable lovers lost
for love played false:
blue music of skies erased,
at one phone-call,
by high fidelity pain.

And what of those friends lost,
children who haven't been born,
how count the cost?
I pick my way alone through the skies,
coldly, still conscious of
that missing splendour
of those once-present stars –
the holes loss makes in its lace of frost –
somewhere between
the lightning and thunder of mourning.

Rupert M. Loydell

Tangerine Dream

for Dad

As synthesizers conjure musical space
I remember how this intrigued you most
out of all the music I played you as a boy.

You were fascinated by the abstraction,
the loops and echoes of new sounds
layered across rhythm and pulse,

said it reminded you of a film you'd seen:
Scott of the Antarctic; and I, having always
been fascinated by the race to the Pole, concurred.

You didn't race for death, it took a little time.
But beside me in this icy emptiness
I remember your tilted head, you listening awhile.

(An eternity away, I sense you smile.)

Jonathan Steffen
Apprentice and Master

All these long years, it had been there for him –
Some patch of canvas naked as the light,
Left untouched by some curious oversight,
Or just abandoned at some patron's whim;
And all the while he'd seen in every space –
As one might see it in a starry sky,
Or in a fire, or water rushing by –
The features of his own first angel's face.
So when at last the master gave him leave
To finish off a corner of one scene,
The pupil had no picture to conceive;
For in that instant, wild and serene,
The angel wings in his own heart unfurled –
His soul his brush, and in his brush the world.

Doris Corti

Devon

Here, in choirs of gulls, soft burr of voices,
here at the shell-sucked pebble ridge,
I choose to die, away from the suburbs
where all day I see symbols – a solitary magpie,
cracked mirrors in cloakrooms, or in the evening a figure
watching over the card player's shoulder.
Middle finger and first I cross, assuaging my own terror.

Here, as an adopted child of its patterns
I feel at the centre, as if simply being was a final acceptance.
Here I can reverse the order of things, sleep in the light,
walk into the darkness, search
on the sea-scraped shore for fragments of time – shells
and small scrunched pebbles that curl away from my fingers
like living things.

Here, slowly, slowly my thoughts slip into echoing rhythms,
into the living land.

Wendy Bardsley
Heathcliff

Today she dreamed a man, delineated with her pen.
Before the ink was dry his eyelids lifted
and his black eyes shone.
She saw how she had stirred his heart.

His essence issues from the wind,
familiars; shadows, briars, the precipice;
his foot's a hoof.

His heartbeat comes within the body of a hawk.
Pen, paper, ink and thought have caught him,
tied him into words; a wretched animal, enraged
and cast within a trap.
And she, a wrist that rubs against a broken pane of glass,
and says the spirit's gist is also warm, at last.

She dreams too fast, invokes the unborn dead.
And spirit touches flesh too much and cymbals clash,
and love is dashed, and roars the moor,
a hound possessed; a fiend,
its bloody gore a savageness she rides.

And the hawk's beak satisfies, to peck the eyes of pain.
It scales the cliff.
What need of flesh? Her spirit soars!

The owl screeches, and the night falls fast.
Curtainless, her window points the way to stars.
They too are rooted into rock, and gleam
an otherness, that seems like love.

Michael Donaghy
Drill

You will do the very last thing.
Wait then for a noise in the chest,
between depth charge and gong,
like the seadoors slamming on the car deck.
Wait for the white noise and the cold astern
and the harbour bobbing and shrinking
into the dark until it's as brilliantly
tiny as the blip when you switch off the telly.
You'll code, a noise like a phone off the hook.

Look down over the rim of the enormous lamp.
Observe the skilled frenzy of the physicians,
a nurse's bald patch, blood. These will blur,
as sure as you've forgotten the voices
of your childhood friends, or your toys,
or, you may note with mild surprise,
your name. For the face they now cover
is a stranger's and it always has been.
Turn away. We commend you to the light,
Where all reliable accounts conclude.

John Heath-Stubbs
A Memory of the Thirties

Of course I'd heard of it – the poverty, hunger marches
The ignominy of the dole, the cruelty of the means test –
But hardly actual in our southern counties,
Our middle class townships. With other young people,
Before Christmas I'd go carol singing,

In aid of what were termed 'the distressed areas',
In ill-defined regions – Tyneside or South Wales.
In large houses we would be asked in, and offered
Mince pies and hot drinks.

Yet a touch of the shadow
Fell over all of us. My father,
Dying by inches could not be a breadwinner; my mother
Daily slaved herself into exhaustion,
Keeping things together with her teaching;
Worry over small price differentials –
Nothing wasted, nothing thrown away;
Clothes patched and repatched.

And that cool day of early autumn
I saw a young man – not more than thirty –
(Probably less, but hunger had pinched him –
He could have had a wife and young children)
Singing or begging for pennies in the street.
His jacket was buttoned up in front,
But at his neck and throat I was aware
He wore no shirt beneath it. He had no shirt.

A provincial reader of rather old-fashioned
Poetry, I hadn't encountered
What were then the slick new school –
Modish revolutionaries, with their drawing-room Karl Marx;
Nor had I taken on board
The sexual mores of some of them.

But as I gazed at that young man
I felt a stab of pity and of shame,
While in my blood, my sixteen-year old blood,
Within whose torrent the hormones hopped and fizzed,
There stirred a craving for the naked flesh
Beneath the jacket and the threadbare trousers.

Paul Greene
Overkill

My mail is like a telephone directory
Of suffering.
Under Ethiopia I have starved
I have heard the scream
Of falling trees under Amazonia
I have felt the earth cracking with drought
Under Botswana and Sudan.

I have banqueted off distress
In many flavours
I have tapped pavements
With a white stick
Have gone submissively to my harpooning
And been recycled to pain daily
As an exploited donkey.
I have inhaled the stench
Of my cigarette burns
As a political dissenter.
I have been variously diseased
And I have laboured
Under grievous disadvantages.
Earthquakes have crushed me
Floods have drowned me
Yes I have responded roundly
To you charities.

But I have to tell you
You have downed all my milk of human kindness
Wrung out my bank account
And left me paupered of emotion.
I no longer heed your teeth gnawing my doormat
I brought my heart to the party
And now it needs re-stringing.

David Perman
November 11th 1979
(60 years after the first Remembrance Day)

The silence is slipped between the hit tunes
like old cheese in a crispbread sandwich
with the scraping of a tang-ey bugle
to make it more palatable.
But it's not silence of course –
there's 'atmosphere', a discreet cough
from an engineer to show the equipment's functioning
and what's a two minutes' silence
when you hear it revving along on the car stereo?
At one time, everything stopped.
Men stood by the car doors, trilbys doffed,
Grandad erect near the wireless, children's heads bowed
waiting for the boom of the guns from Land's End
to John O'Groats.
Anyone who moved was a traitor.
But that was before Wonderful Radio One
before disc jockeys and Caroline
before the Beatles, the Stones, Bob Dylan and
Jimmy Hendrix.
Even before Bill Hayley. But we still do it,
the two-minute memory not for the
Kampuchean dead or Afghanistan or the Ogaden
not even for Belfast, Aden, Arnhem and the Imjon.
It's only for the kids of Flanders
senseless to the strong beat of the Big Bertha Band
whose youth culture fertilised the poppies
in the unsilent mud.

Beryl Cross
War Generations

His father saw Dunkirk and Alamein,
Defeat and victory,
As did his enemy.
Both knew the fear, the triumph and the pain,
Staccato notes of gunshots, bombs' red rain.

His grandfather had watched his comrades die
In rat-infested trench,
Had smelt the corpses' stench
From friend and foe under a Flanders' sky,
Survived mud, mustard gas and dysentery.

His great-grandfather fought in Zulu wars,
Witnessed the warrior-bands
In Cetewayo's lands,
Faced spear-forests, froze to the cry that soars
For blood-lust, disbelieved his country's cause.

His direct ancestor at Waterloo,
Deafened by cannon-fire,
Horse-trampled in the mire,
Hauled himself up. remounted, charging through
Napoleon's lines, his sabre slashing true.

His forebears of the seventeenth century
Chose King and Parliament.
As was the nation rent
So was his family – cousin to see
Sword-thrust through cousin, bloodily.

Now, within Bosnia, ferrying aid
To enclaved towns, one shot,
One sniper's bullet, hot
With death, smashes his windscreen; crimson-sprayed
That night on television screens displayed.

R.S. Thomas

Two Views of a Gorilla

We confront one another,
a meeting not of minds
but of fingers. Is it sadness
I imagine on his gnarled
face, sadness for the failure
to catch up, sadness rather
for what I have become,
a brother who has put him
behind bars, when all he asks
of me is that I love him?
When two such contemplate
each other, which is made monster
by the bars that are between them?

Dying she put out a finger
in my direction; trembling
I touched it. The gorilla,
postponing the death of the species
behind bars, puts out a hand, too,
which I take, putting the stars
in a frenzy. All over the night
sky their alarm rings,
warning of the danger
that, in all the emptiness
around, when two creatures
meet, they can come so close
via the emotions to meaning.

Danielle Hope
Bad Tenant

This week I am another's life:
borrow scarves, socks, books,
even new waking hours.
Rise at noon, stay up late,
drink whiskey she cannot bear.

Bad tenant. I swore
at her bank manager, accountant, boss.
I won't take her messages now,
answer the 'phone, the door.
I grin at the neighbour
she hates, starve her fish.

What did she ever get
from her shoe-boxed life?
Bothered by dreamed up nails
seeing adders in grass snakes,
bindweed in hare-bells.

Next week she'll be back.
Checking the mail for cheques,
counting the empty bottles,
full ashtrays, stains on the wall.
But out in the coppice bulbs grow,
ignoring us both.

William Oxley
The White Table, 4 am.

You are asleep my hope-and-all
in the guest room above the night wind
while I, at the white table,
ponder nervous sounds of yet another night,
a wakeful speck of metropolitan thought.

It is the hour of the burglar
and the anxious father, of late lovers
and tragic drinkers – and we
who shuffle the endless pack of words
share the fever and fret of them all.

There is no silence outside the mind
but revealing noise: the bitty tick of clock
scratching the wall, the wailing
identity of police cars pursuing
their morality through suburban dreams,

and, if I listen hard enough,
beyond the screams of insecurity – no,
not the scrunching of death's heel
on gravel! – but something more: always
the murmur of impossible truth, blank
and white as this table on which I write.

Golders Green, 22.10.94.

Myra Schneider
Leavetaking

And when he was struck speechless
then I wanted him to speak again,
when he couldn't deliver the orders
I wanted to cram back into his mouth,
break the unbearable waters
of wrath over my head
then I wanted to hear his voice again,
would have held out cupped hands
for a command, a judgement, a complaint.

When he was sentenced
to a wordless struggle for breath
and could no longer devour us
with: 'I'm dying: I wish I was dead,'
I discovered what I'd guessed;
he'd cried wolf instead of pain,
stalked by implacable terrors
he dared not name. But he'd given
doctors instructions to haul him
back for the last mile, last inch

to keep tabs on the world,
its disgraceful conduct of itself,
his daughters' failings, successes
and the complex finances in his head.
Minutes before his lungs
finally rebelled
his fingers plotted in the air
the upward curve of a grandson's career.

And in those four speechless days
when his eyes fixed

on the precise saline drip
drip through glass arteries,
when his hands washed themselves
of the universe or clutching at a pen
produced strange new writing,
did a kind of acceptance trickle through?

In those four speechless days
I began to strip him of shortcomings,
bury the terrible damages
and I hung onto his zest,
his generosities, his ever-
enquiring scientific mind,
his hunger for consciousness,
that miracle each person carries,
a delicate globe lit
by intricate, unseen filaments
which is so suddenly put out,
which is totally
irreplaceable.

Ian Caws

Clarinet

On yellow gardens, the whispering rain,
And I am up at the Big House again
Watching an autumn sky drift in the lake.
Between trees, a miniature Greek temple
Provides lovers with shelter and deer look
Upwind, the first to sense the weather's pull.

In a marquee, the town band is playing
Beatle songs but I will not be staying
To see the boy on first clarinet meet
His father who approaches through the park.
Always he approaches, in that minute
When winter's fingers turn the landscape dark.

On charcoal coloured gardens, a sharp rain,
And I am in the Saxon church again
Listening to the town band. And a boy
Who has not brought his clarinet will hear
A different harmony and obey
A stranger rhythm, having come to where

No one presumes to play the melody.
Between pillars, light shifts in a moody
Way and there is no shelter for a boy
In a father's death. Only in the wet
On Sundays, when the town band takes its bow,
Rougher hands pull apart his clarinet

Michael Croshaw
'The Waste Land' as a Sonnet

Once April's gone, that time of mixed impressions,
We seek the Son of Man in rock and stone
But, finding only fear, try tarot sessions
And horoscopes for Mrs. Equitone.
From meeting Stetson, I return to you.
Your nerves being bad, I drain a public glass
Then walk the unreal city (pausing to view
Typist and lover), like Tiresias.

Moorgate – Margate – Carthage – why should I want
To remember now Phlebas is dead and thunder calls
The Buddha's sermon from here to Himavant
And night is thick with bats and blackened walls?

As bridge and tower fall, Hieronymo's mad.
I shore fragments and quote an Upanishad.

Christopher J.P. Smith
The Partial Resurrection of St. Medrawt Mor

See that squint-eyed fellow with the cockerel's head
Lounging in the bar like Hell and leather?
Once, they say, he was a man
Something similar to us even.
But a man, how shall I say, greater, taller,
With a voice,
A steeple of bells, a speechmaker
Yes, he had power in his words
A hero beating the anvil for its muddy sparks
Or anyone caught between his cock and fists.
Once I overheard them, the women he had pierced,
Hundreds, gathered in an oak grove,
All asking for blood,
His blood –
Yet anyone of them would have run to him
For one lift of an eyebrow or upraised arm.
Those shoulders you can just make out
Under the fur and bandages –
Their wonderful brownskin man
A voice on the rooftree with hands clasped at the moon,
Shook down the stars to dust on his knuckles,
Took Troy to Helen and killed Hector.
Left Dido sitting in ash, burnt London,
Made a pie from Grendel and his Dam
Then ate it.
Would not kneel to the white Christ for any gold
Yet wept at a sparrow caught in a trap.
And look
There is that great rusty bloody sword
Balanced over his knees
That no man has broken in this light
Or in any tale we've told.

Lotte Kramer

Subjunctive

I wonder, had you lived
Into my married years,
Become a grandmother,
A mother-in-law.
Would we have stayed
As closely bound?

Would you have understood
My terrors, doubts,
The years of searching,
Feeling my way
For yet another thought.
Another creed, perhaps?

Would you've been tolerant
Of my rejection of the old
Considered insufficient then,
Or turned away in grief,
Been disappointed
In your daughter's treason?

Would I have run to you
When life-lines changed
Love to a spider's web,
Or kept it hidden
In my ghetto's night,
Afraid to burden you?

John Gurney
Haiku

Ah, the sheer beauty
of this Emptiness
beneath the speeding seasons!

Swallows dipping wings
into the lake. Circles move
through one another.

And now the trees, like
thin deciduous women, strip
themselves for winter.

Look. Something out of
nothing. Down the asphalt, snow,
like apple-petals!

Sebastian Barker

The Sage Of The Cambrian Mountains

Tramp the hills, old sage, the chapel there
Is stones the rains now whip with merciless
Lashes. The mortar's all dissolved. Once sacred air
Now kills the strong foundations where you learnt to bless.

There's nothing left. The hills are lost in rain.
The antique yew lies rotting in the grass.
The flaking graves say nothing about pain.
There's nothing left. And nothing, too, will pass.

Slowly the clouds co-operate with night
To freeze the lakes. The winds do not relent.
This is the way of life. And it is right
You tramp the hills, old sage, with sage intent.

Blitzed by the blizzard, long morning helps you stand
Snowy-haired in snow, with one uplifted hand.

Lotte Moos

Flitting Rhyme

Years – heartbeats and all – morticed to stone
Fears – domestic voles – gnawing at bone
Tears – ingrown splinters – are here on loan

Spun by the hungry years' thumb
Hardship's cement churns in the drum
Till, ground into one,
Both house and you
Are 'adjourned'

And the bailiffs come.

Sally Purcell

Untitled

Out from the moon's dark hillside
ghosts drift across our noon-day,
chill the April sun,
rap on windows of dream.
They are forgetting how they ever lived
under this darkness.

And I can scarcely recognise
grief, now levelled by the tide
invading upland gardens,
the fierce immortal sea.

Roger Harvey

Lunchtime Concert: Ancient Music

Tongue your breath into the flute,
Press the reed between your lips,
Voice loud and rich all things once mute,
Bring the harpsichord, string the lute
To rest across your hips.

Thrill me with a rising tide
And press the wood against your throat;
The swollen viol is yours to ride
With cunning fingers, legs astride
You tease with every note.

Shake, take me, slake me – please!
Make sunlight shimmer though the dust.
Grip the bass between your knees,
Beat hot fingers on the keys,
And strum me mad with lust.

I starve and thirst and crave for more:
Set strings a-quiver with wild caress.
Brace bare toes upon the floor,
Play the lady, play the whore
Inside your flowered dress.

With arms and fingers wet my love,
Deftly turn the dotted page;
Bow with hair and sweat my love,
We'll be merry yet my love,
My blood is in a rage.

Burn with laughter, flood with tears,
Thrust the pleasure, grasp the pain.
The life that's born in joys and fears,
That spills and runs down music's years
Will live in us again.

Heather Buck
To the Unborn

I have begun to pray for you,
though only five months in the womb
you are a person I will come to know
when in tomorrow's house you carve
in me a small hollow of love
filled with the joy of seeing you prove
the wind, the rain and the untried snow.

Your body, as yet unfinished, must grow
before we see you whole, complete.
Awaiting your entrance into life, we wish
you health and happiness, but know
all lives are made of dark and light
that in their interplay might wisdom grow.

I hope for nothing more than to hold
your hand when the small rains come,
and pray that we who love you may never
block your light nor wall you with our needs,
but love you enough to let you be
the self you are singularly destined to be.

David Perman

Stubble Burning

It's been an airborne summer
as the binding waters fled
and earth rose up to catch the sun.
All life exists now in the browning,
parched fields, tanned skin,
even enamelled ladybirds
were dust scuffed.
But their bright horde has been sucked away
with the moths and long-legs.
Wasps have come and gone
and now the air is ruled by the sun
and the skeletal ash
from stubble burning.
Before relief comes,
all life will dance in the fire.

David Sutton

Earth to Earth

Forgive me, most faithful lover, I know you're still making
Gifts to me: today in the meadow it was
A burnet moth in its magician's cloak
Of black and crimson; last night, broken cloud
Around a full moon, rainbowed with its burnish.
Forgive me, then, if I seem to look away
Like one embarrassed by what he cannot repay.

If I said that I was tired, would you understand,
You who never grow tired, whose poems unfold
In the soft thick parchment of magnolia petals,
A guaranteed perfection, old as spring?
You have suffered too, but to be a creature divided
Against itself is a thing you have not known.
For you, all's oneness: water, sunlight, stone.

What my own kind want of me, you would understand,
Knowing their ways, to covet, to consume.
They plough the field of my mind, they harrow me
With sharp needs, make their urgent sowings, reap
Their profitable harvests. But you would have me
Only alert, and fallow, listening
In a dry country for the hidden spring.

Once it was easy to return to you:
When I ran like a fox, and the hunt of the world went by
As I lay in your arms, in the breath of summer bracken.
I loved to run at dusk on grass, barefoot,
Palping the planet, till I dropped and lay
Immortal, melded, watching blue air swim,
Feeling the blood bliss throb in every limb.

Those paths close up, or we abandon them.
Need narrows us, till all our ways are one,
But that leads back: bear with me as I bear,
Holding myself still upright, as I must,
Against your green embrace, your gravity.
As fox to earth at last, to grass the dew,
As love to lover, I shall come to you.

Merryn Williams

The Substitute

I shake your hand, sit round the crowded table,
knowing there's work, as always, to get through.
Outside, I talk about our brave new leader,
tell them you're very gifted (and it's true),
play the admiring friend. That's hard to do
when instinct howls, it shouldn't have been you.

Sometimes my voice frays and my eyes betray me
at the day's end. Impossible to hide
gut feelings, though we're both polite – extremely.
You'd not be here, if someone hadn't died.
Still other times, my mind roams backwards, to
the man whose place you took (worth ten of you).

You've changed, you've got that golden glaze of power
since your huge stroke of luck. Oh, yes, I knew
what thoughts went through your mind, when I and others
wept, couldn't think what we were going to do.
My mind blanks out. I haven't got a clue
why he died first, when it should have been you.

Joe Hackett
For a Murder Victim

The city's muscles still quiver
long after its lights are switched off.

Restless streets twitch and shake,
parks stretch in the moonglow.

A word passes from one suburb to another.
"Murder," whispers a tower block, "bloody murder."

"Another," sighs a terrace to a square
and violence clings to the wings of pigeons
rising in fright then gliding down,
murder, murder, until
on the morning hour of four the word's last echo
is sucked down a sewer,
swept under jaundiced streets
into the chocolate-coloured river out to sea,

leaving the city quiet at last, clutching its corpse
as the moon sinks into darkness, darkness till dawn.

Sebastian Barker
Double Take

There's another world mixed in with this one.
You see it when someone dies.
The holy spirit of life and death
And the monumental lies.

Fred Beake

The Light

The road divides. Her heart-light flickers on.
Down which road? It is too uncertain.

A distant light, which might be just the moon
catches trees along the steep way down.

Another flickers in and out
as on some hidden lane a tractor thrusts its snout.

But where's the light for which I've searched
every hour without end for over thirty years?

I think I see it sometimes beyond a boulder
in the grey moor spaces of the inner mind.

I think I see it sometimes in the brittle day
but everytime I approach it has gone away.

Perhaps if I follow some sky-winding bird
I will find the true point on the card.

Perhaps I grasp where I should find
or am I merely man who cannot see his end?

Surely her presence chimed once with mine,
but since that day I cannot find the tune.

Sin with age makes us all cynical
and our flesh grows brittle.

But still I reach for her, cannot escape
the distant beckoning light.

W.D. Jackson

The Gift of Tongues

(from *Self-portrait as a White-collar*)

The baby sleeps in her dim bed
Like a warm fruit on a summer night,
As plump and full as if she'd fed
On prelapsarian liquid light;
She rocks on a dumb umbilical tree –
Or so I think of her as we

Relax of a Sunday afternoon,
Listening to music while howling snow
Is hurled outside our window. Soon
The spring will come. But now we go
Lying enarmed, enlegged together
Beyond the wordless rage of the weather –

And beyond the raging words of a world
Where minds are bought and sold to their harm,
Where men and bits of paper are hurled
In a windless, eyeless, endless storm,
Which cannot give, which thinks it can take,
Which can only undo, uproot, unmake

The fragile fruit of infancy,
Till the cold woman and the loud-mouthed man
Can only gain in innocency
By luck or some well- or ill-laid plan ...
My blood feels crumpled, cold, but your hand
Coaxes it quietly to a stand ...

I have been suffering all this week
From a tongue gone brittle earning its bread
By chopping words. Your curious lick

Raises me from clattering dead,
But your back's still tense. Our silent sex
Fits my concave to your convex

Which I gently stroke and warm with my palms
Till, moving down beneath the covers
I feel you slowly soften. My arms
Encircle flesh which only lovers –
Giving and taking with opening holes –
Soothe with their tongues and tongue with their souls.

Michael Donaghy

A Yearbook

If a year is a prayer you're to get by heart,
It's far and away too long.
If its days are a rhyme for remembering,
The words you heard were wrong.
If it were a song you were meant to sing,
It wouldn't be this song. Whereas,
If it's a book in which you read
And are read yourself in turn,
(A big book, say, an expensive book,
In some language you suffer to learn)
The infinite shift of gist within gist
Would make these pages burn. Not that they will,
Not now nor at year's end, not after, nor until.

U.A. Fanthorpe

Kinch & Lack

(Boys' Outfitters)

Elderly man with a tape-measure.
Pedantic; a shade arch
(I don't see this at the time),
Treats my brother like a bride.

My mother not at ease
(I feel, but don't know why);
My brother, flattered, diffident,
Somehow aware of destiny.

Youngest son faces his kingdom
And his trousseau, socks, cap, scarf.
Wreathed in official colours
For unimagined deeds.

Greek, rugger, chemistry, things
He will do and I shan't,
Though I am two years older,
Taller, have read more books.

He's rehearsed for a special future
By a man with pins in his mouth;
Seven-year Dante, whose Vergil
Salutes his inches with respectful craft.

Mother stands restlessly by,
The cheque-book in her bag,
(And I know, without being told,
There's a world enlisting him
That hasn't a place for me.

O.K. I'll make my own).

Austin Cooper
Seamus Heaney's Return
to Ireland after his presentation with the Nobel Prize for Literature

Did he have that excitement of every return,
Seeing the blue rising of the Dublin Mountains,
Hearing the trumpeting of stags in the West?
But certainly aware of that vivid green.
His aeroplane nosing out of thin cloud
Above Ireland's Eye and Howth, down
To Dublin ... and then he at the door
Hatless with baggy trousers, portly
With shy faun-like smile and humorous eyes
To receive a kiss from a beautiful woman,
The President of Ireland herself alone
And all most naturally, arm in arm
With her, walking ... who could want better,
A welcome not even given to royalty.

All manner of Irishman was there to greet
'God bless you!' and a hurry to match his pace
And talk with him in laughter ... touch a sleeve,
Ireland's poet come safely home, worthy
Successor to immortal Yeats but with easy touch ...
I, rightly, forgot I only liked
His verses half as well ...
It was an Occasion!

Sophie Hannah

Preventative Elegy

There will not be a burial,
There will not be a wake.
No ashes will be sprinkled
Over the stream or lake.
There won't be a cremation
A coffin or a shroud.
No hearse will park along the road –
Your death is not allowed.

There will not be a graveyard,
There'll be no marble stone
Bearing a carved endearment.
No flesh will shrink to bone
And in the town that loves you
There'll be no sobbing crowd.
No-one inherits anything –
Your death is not allowed.

No grief will need to be disguised
As just a bit upset.
No-one will wonder whether to
Remember or forget
Or which would cause the greater pain,
And whether we laughed or rowed
Last time will be irrelevant –
Your death is not allowed.

Others will die instead of you.
A fixed amount must die
(If there are quotas with these things)
And strangers' wives will cry

But I will have no need to say
I loved you and was proud
To be what I have been to you –
Your death is not allowed.

Jonathan Steffen

Caveat

Beware of those who learn their love from books –
Suppliers of the apposite quotation,
Providers of the perfect explanation
The man of lesser reading overlooks.
Beware the magic of the borrowed word –
The lines that ring so fine through unknown lives,
The undreamt harmonies the poet contrives,
That on your lips will simply sound absurd.
There are no teachers for the lover's heart,
No theorists or gurus who can guide
The student in this labyrinthine art –
An art eternal in its infancy,
Which has to stumble at each hopeful stride.
Go your own way. And fall. That's constancy.

Pauline Stainer

The Inspiriting

The white tree
is silence, parting
like many waters.

What kindles the trance
a flock of waxwings
alighting

their continuous song
an extension of the wind
in the branches

petals falling
with slow vertigo
and time not passing.

Wendy Cope

Unwritten Rules

Assonance, consonance, they are OK –
You can rhyme nut with bug, you can rhyme it with bat –
But full rhyme's a little bit suspect today.

Reverse rhyme or pararhyme: far more cachet –
Rhyme bottom with boggle, or rhyme knit with gnat.
Assonance, consonance, they are OK,

And much easier too. There's an endless array
Of near-rhymes, a limit to full rhymes with splat,
And full rhyme's a little bit suspect today.

New Formalists rhyme in the US of A,
The poetic establishment dons its high hat.
Assonance, consonance, they are OK.

A trendsetting poet was once heard to say
You can rhyme knife with fork. I'm not sure about that
But full rhyme's a little bit suspect today.

It's important to write in an up-to-date way
And I trust it is clear that I know where it's at:
Assonance, consonance, they are OK
But full rhyme's a little bit suspect today.

John Burnside
August

I must have imagined the time, going south,
when we drove into a Lammas festival.
I'd been asleep; then woke to a flicker of lights
and children's faces; candles; wisps of straw;
the whole town abroad in the dusk
like their people before them.

Some border town, I think:
three churches and a bank, a tidy square,
the one hotel with views across the park
to friendly hills,
its phantom inhabitants clinging to what they knew
from habit, or some half-remembered time
of magic, when a bright god stepped away
and left them to wind and rain, and the slow fade of apples.

Kathleen McPhilemy
Redundancies

What has happened to the boys?
Young women with wideawake eyes
come and go through opening doors;
they have such poise,
proud possessors of the actual world:
but what of the boys?

Cyber warriors, heroes of hyperreality
earphone-sealed from the actual world
they slouch from school to the corner;
or, fit for nothing,
pump themselves up for a life without work.
Look at the boys:
woolly hats pulled down round their eyes
warm the space where their butterfly brains
flitter and shift to the flick of a switch.

What is it destroys,
and when does it happen, the light in their eyes?
nursery, puberty or the moment they see
their father with no job, their mother with two:
What have we done to the boys?

Jane Kirwan

Looking at the River

With watercolour
only the absence
suggests its depth
like the colourless centre
of a flame
or that silence
that space with no breath
no heart beat
before you tell me.

Ruth Bidgood

Characters

Why can't they stay in their categories?
Look out for the clown with the knife!
Here they come, capering, wombling,
dancing, skipping and stumbling,
these hordes of inconsistencies,
blurry-lined ambiguities,
chancy, unstable, playing merry hell
with planning and preconception, spoiling
notions of nature and plot, foiling
attempts at pattern, tumbling pell-mell,
full of muddled rebellious life.

Tim Liardet

High Wire

With inner calm, nerve, a perfect assurance
of body and mind he of the furrowed soles
is sliding up the steeply rising wire without a pole

fifty feet in the air, while clowns fifty feet below
follow as if to catch, as if to prove him fallible.
Up there, to the drum roll, the spotlight's circle

against a kitsch and starry firmament can blow
his equally balletic shadow three times
his size, pinned delicately by a toe;

so far beneath, the praise in our sound
comes from those of us who only with much practice
walk straight without a pole on the ground.

Christopher North

That Which Is Lost

The Estonian translated poems from the T'ang
and later in a village birch grove
were found the fresh corpses of two phrases
that clarified the texture of pines ascending
the sides of a misty caldera.

The professor of Russian literature in Salzburg
revered the Estonian and translated
his studies of ancient Chinese
and later the body of a birch grove
was found in the shadows beneath a black poplar.

A Californian poet, the professor's student,
translated his work on that unheard of Estonian
for the new magazine "Haight-Ashbury Runner"
and some remains found beside Malibu palm boles
were recognizably trees but of what species

no-one could tell.

Debjani Chatterjee

From the Base

Easy to succumb to Kali Yuga.*
relive our nightmares, accepting defeat;
but this is not the way to scale the heights.

Action – collective or single – creates,
give no dumb assent to self-destruction,
we are our own avatars in this age.

Time's cyclic wheel is not the enemy
when our breath can turn it anti-clockwise.
Drawn stick-figures, we have fleshed beyond the frame.

Reflection shapes us, our feelings flower;
we raise questions, regardless of answers:
what crowns the summit is not our concern.

Born at the base, our eyes must search upwards,
our natural response to step forward.

Kali Yuga or the Dark Age presages the final destruction of this world cycle.

Eunice De Souza

Pilgrim

The hills crawl with convoys.
Slow lights wind round
and down the dark ridges
to yet another
termite city.

The red god rock
watches all that passes.
He spoke once.
The blood-red boulders
are his witness.

God rock, I'm a pilgrim.
Tell me –
Where does the heart find rest?

Fred Beake

Burnham Beeches

When the winds blow at Burnham Beeches
and remove the gold leaves from the trees
there will still be that terrible quiet

and the sound of the fall of single leaves
as loud and final as anything military
in the adjoining regions of our minds.

Catherine Fisher

Amnesia

I can't remember if I used to come here.
There's a picture of Our Lady in a drawer,

old, well-fingered. I could ask Isabelle
but won't. Leaning here feels

good, it feels right, and suddenly I know
that you and I have never been apart; I remember you

in the fragments of the car, the white room
when I woke. The silence, the strange calm.

I should be angry with you, stand up and shout,
but the sun's in the windows and out-

side the ice-cream van is playing silly tunes.
Give me time. I may understand,

not hurt so much. Here come the girls,
pattering up the marble in their sandals.

Is it you who sends the sparks, the pictures
of people I don't know, the bitter

longing some smells can bring? Will you bless
the secret joy inside the loss?

John Burnside

A Photograph of Old West Fife

I'm thinking of when you could buy
returns
      Of buses that no longer run
beyond the cemetery to glittering
alleys of beech mast and moss
                    Of towns that no longer
figure on the maps
            Of thin men printed in coal
on a misted glass
        Of Geraldine
Cecilia
        Yvonne
            Of Gala Days
                    Of turning around
and smelling the wind off the Forth
on Stenhouse Street
                I'm thinking of myself
of picking the leaves from a wall
of privet and tasting the sap
of wading across the burn at Fulford bridge
my sandals filling with water, my bare feet
chilled to the bone
            Of darkness and the echo in the woods
come out to touch my face and make me strange
an arm's length away from the dead
or a mile from home.

Alan Hester

You Never Walk Alone

It's a counterfeit childhood
That has you under house arrest,
The withheld freedom of these precious years
A victim of my adult fears.

You can't ride your bike to your friend's house,
Spend summer in the fields,
Catch buses into town
Or waste your evenings hanging around.

There's no making your own mistakes,
No little gangs or hideaways,
No playing in the street till late,
No venturing beyond the garden gate.

I'm angry for you, angry with myself,
Accomplice in the theft of freedoms
That should be yours by right,
Not given up like this without a fight.

Where can you go in private
To be horrid to your sister?
Where can you sit and do nothing
And no-one ask you if you're bored?

You must think a nutter's waiting
At every corner, that cars will aim for you.
Even the school bangs home its slogans –
Say No To Strangers: Stranger – Danger.

You don't do the things I did,
You never have adventures of your own.
You can't escape this gilded cage,
You never walk alone.

Michael Henry
Roadside Shrine

I saw him flag down a motorist
like the griefleader in Greek tragedy.
I heard his words: 'Please help my dying wife.'

I saw the wife was dying as they lifted
the ballast of her body into the ambulance.
I saw them lay a cold white blanket
on her husband who'd been killed outright.

I heard them at the hospital
bearing witness bible-mouthed,
their horror at the incident
mitigated by envy of such love.

A guardian ghost. Orpheus returning
from the afterworld in casual dress.
I remember hawkweed at the roadside
and rays of sunshine in the Arctic light.

Holding up my love for my own wife,
I shall expect a new Catholic feast-day
for the miracle of their coming back.

Helen Dunmore

We are Men, not Beasts

We are men, not beasts,
though we fall in the dark
on the rattlesnake's path
and flinch with fire of fear
running over our flesh
and beat it to death,

We are men, not beasts
and we walk upright
with the moss-feathered dark
like a shawl on our shoulders
and we carry fire
steeply, inside a cage of fingers,

we are men, not beasts,
and what we cannot help wanting
we banish – the barn yawn, the cow breath,
the stickiness we come from.

Hugo Williams
Alternator

To be in possession of the facts, yet powerless,
is new to me, a strange technology
of waiting, weighing possibilities,
watching the dud decisions
fizzing and popping in the night,
like this moth-crazed street light,
its opposite poles rigged to an alternator
of breaking up or asking her to marry me.

I make my heart beat, remembering her silences.
My brains fly out through the top of my head.
Run to the ends of the earth?
Or set up camp on her doorstep?
I take my place on her answering tape.
My innocent enquiries. My carefree messages.
'The phone was ringing when I came in ...
I was wondering if you'd got my letter ...'

Me

How am I feeling this morning?
Or is it too early to say?
I check by swallowing
to see if my throat's still sore.
I check by thinking
to see if my brain still hurts.

I'm walking along out of doors,
not feeling anything much,
when it suddenly comes to me:
I don't feel so bad anymore.
I think to myself,
I'll soon put a stop to that!'

Ross Cogan

Whisky Priest

'Imagine a tapestry', he had once said.
'Viewed from the back what is it but a mess
of stitches, knots and loops and broken thread
hanging on rough cloth? We couldn't guess
the pattern until we'd turned it round. Or then
there's television. Close its points of light,
and the full picture only emerges when
we back away.' Adages that sound trite

in my mouth now impressed me when he spoke
and swilled a dust of Oxford through the air.
Later he nonplussed me with a joke
about how hard his vows had been to bear.
Before I could understand years had to pass;
the world unravel, darkly, through a glass.

John Heath-Stubbs

Ten Kinds of Birds

(for John and Hammond Minihan)

Ten kinds of birds I have identified
By their calls and songs as we sit here
Under a darkening sky of June, drinking our wine.
First the wheezing call of the greenfinch
Met me on my arrival;
The robin redbreast, that sang to us
The long Winter through, is hardly trying now –
I guess his brood is fledged and flown;
From a fruit tree near the house –
Unpretentious – that's the garden warbler.
The sparrow's only got one note – but he's working on it.
More eloquent the blackbird – two blackbirds
With adjoining territories – one answers,
But not identically, the other's phrases –
Sweet and rich their songs. More shrill, more passionate,
A little way off, a thrush is singing also;
Further, at a copse's edge,
The foolish croodling of the wood-pigeon.

From the church tower, time to time
A party of jackdaws flies. They cruise around for a bit,
Then return, chattering,
As is their custom: 'Let's all keep together, boys,
If there's a hawk around
She'll likely pick off a straggler.'
Now the not-quite-English accents
Of the collared dove, somewhere to the right.
It seems he woke a chaffinch up,
Who repeated his rattling tattle,
Ending with the phrase that sounds like: 'Ginger beer'

And then fell silent. So it goes on and on
Till one by one sleep claims the birds
As it must soon claim us, and we go in.
There is one last blackbird. With sombre plume
And golden mouth, he flings his melody
Into the Darkness –
So let it be with me, when the night comes.

Leah Fritz

Long Distance

'This is the MCI operator, calling
from the United States.' My own voice jumps
an octave. Co-conspirator, I tell him
you're not here (no lies). We've done
this act for years: Person-to-person, you ask
for yourself, and then I phone direct. Cheap
and cheerful conversation. Now you've gone back
again – strange to say 'home'. Way down deep
old ghost of a cord refuses to break, insists
that where I am is where you still belong,
not half-way round the world. Now, as if
I'm talking to myself, I hear your strong
American accents, your West-Coast-hardened Rs
(that's new) against my English-quickened ear,
reminder that we both have travelled far
and you are safe and home is anywhere.

So tenuous this line. Our faceless words
convey so little. My tightening throat can't cope
with such high registers. Absurd, that chord,
this cord, this fibre-optic cable, hope.

Ruth Padel

Falling

This isn't happening

Play it down
Dress it in Levis or a babygro

Buy it a hamburger
Buy it a drink

Put it out with the cat
Make a credit card arrangement
With the taxidermist on Upper Street

Book it a package deal
Where icicles go

For their holiday in spring
This isn't happening

And it's doing it so fast.

The Eyes

When he came down from the platform
And walked out,
Everyone clapping,

His eyes as he passed her were proud
And shy of being proud

And glad she was there.
She was a lightning photographer
Handed the secret of storms.

Dannie Abse

An Interrupted Letter

In this room's winterlight the travail of
a letter to a new widow. Solemn,
the increasing enterprise of age.
I stutter. Consoling words come slow,
seem false, as if spoken on a stage.
It would be easier to send flowers.

I think of her closing her husband's eyelids
and I look up. Siberian snow hesitated,
then parachuted into our garden
for hours, confiscating yesterday's
footprints. Shall I send flowers?

But now my wife, unaware in the far kitchen,
suddenly sings, captivating me,
my pen mid-air above a muffled page.

When we were young, tremulant with Spring,
often off-key she'd sing her repertoire –
dateless folksongs, dance tunes dated.
In her Pears-suds bath I'd hear her,
in the Morris Minor with our kids.

I must return to my hiemal letter.
Sing on love, as once you did, sing and sing
for past youth, for hungers unabated.

Anne Born

Red Wine Pantoum

Red wine is the blood of the sun
bled from vined veins of grapes
those bubbles of the flesh that come
like little worlds   perfect shapes.

Bled from vined veins of grapes
decanted into a cask of wood
little worlds   perfect shapes
liquefied for joy and good.

Decanted into a cask of wood
and left to sleep away from air
liquefied for joy and good
waiting for a foot on the stair.

Left to sleep away from air
until poured in a hand-cut glass
waiting for a foot on the stair
to let the sunlight in at last.

Poured in a hand-cut glass
raised high to start the singing
to let the sunlight in at last
lift hearts and send them soaring.

Raised high to start the singing
those bubbles of the flesh that come
to lift hearts and send them soaring.
Red wine is the blood of the sun

Maureen Kenchington
Lying Parallel

What lies between us
now that the dust has settled?
Looking back, I can see the path we took
from friendship to love;
how can we ever retrace those steps?
When we talked of commitment,
you crossed your fingers. Behind your back
I gave you my word, but
can't deny there was someone else involved.
It was never serious. You said you
were so much in love with me, but
I chose to believe you
didn't really mean it. Like a fool,
I didn't begin to understand you.

I didn't begin to understand you
didn't really mean it. Like a fool
I chose to believe you
were so much in love with me, but
it was never serious, you said. You
can't deny there was someone else involved!
I gave you my word, but
you crossed your fingers behind your back
when we talked of commitment.
How can we ever retrace those steps
from friendship to love?
Looking back, I can see the path we took
now that the dust has settled.
What lies between us!

Ken Smith

In the Next Street

There's only ever one argument: his,
bawling out whoever punctuates
the brief intervals his cussing
interrupts, something unheard, reason perhaps.

What you never get is silence,
always some groan on the horizon
out on the borders of attention
where would be quiet if they let it.

Always some conversation far away,
foreign, banal, dramatic, translated
it means *my wife's name is Judit.*
I am an engineer from Spidertown.

What to reply? *Your Majesty,*
my name is Smith. All lies anyway,
all we do is get drunk, the evening's end
collapsing loosely into gutturals.

We drink to silence, where the stars think.
We drink to the music of rain on the roof.
We drink to mothers, brothers, lovers, kids,
to the candle burning down its length

till someone blows it out. Distance
makes no difference, the same want
for love or money, the numbers of the winning line
in the state lottery like a needle in the brain.

And then I've had enough. I want
to go home now, far away, plug myself
back into the sockets, the blackbird,
the evening humming stories to itself.

Everything in its place, the moths,
the mouse in the mousetrap. And
in the next street the same old argument.
He's sure he's right.

Leah Fritz

Solstice: Winter

(i.m. Anita Hoffman)

Meanwhile a friend is dying, cell by cell.
A fog-edged moon that's overstayed the night
beckons through black trees. Magnet-eyed,
it draws long buried rivers in its swell.
Low in the east, the sun stands still. Wind serrates
glass, yet she persists with life. This is
Fall's final curtain call. Infinite twists
permute a trite, exhausted theme: Death waits –
art's in the kill. Though tortures disease invents
inquisitors must envy, and nature incites
her marrow to rebel, she wills this rite
prolonged, this morning/night when sun suspends
its motion, moon cancels flight, the cutting wind
engraves the sharded crystal of her mind.

161

Kona Macphee

IVF

I come home early, feel the pale house close
around me as the pressure of my blood
knocks at my temples, feel it clench me in
its cramping grasp, the fierceness of its quiet
sanctioning the small and listless hope
that I might find it mercifully empty.

Dazed, I turn the taps to fill the empty
tub, and draw the bathroom door to close
behind me. I lie unmoving, feel all hope
leaching from between my legs as blood
tinges the water, staining it the quiet
shade of a winter evening drifting in

on sunset. Again, no shoot of life sprouts in
this crumbling womb that wrings itself to empty
out the painfully-planted seeds. The quiet
doctors, tomorrow, will check their notes and close
the file, wait for the hormones in my blood
to augur further chances, more false hope.

My husband holds to patience, I to hope,
and yet our clockworks are unwinding. In
the stillness of the house, we hear our blood
pumped by hearts that gall themselves, grow empty:
once, this silence, shared, could draw us close
that now forebodes us with a desperate quiet.

I hear him at the door, but I lay quiet,
as if, by saying nothing, I may hope
that somehow his unknowingness may close
a door on all the darkness we've let in:
the nursery that's seven years too empty;
the old, unyielding stains of menstrual blood.

Perhaps I wish the petitioning of my blood
for motherhood might falter and fall quiet,
perhaps I wish that we might choose to empty
our lives of disappointment, and of hope,
but wishes founder – we go on living in
the shadow of the cliffs now looming close:

the blood that's thick with traitorous clots of hope;
the quiet knack we've lost, of giving in;
the empty room whose door we cannot close.

Anna Adams

The Wood along the River's Bank

for Denis Clinch

This is the church where nature prays
while, ceaselessly whispering rosaries,
the rock-bottom river of boulder-beads
creeps under mossed root buttresses.

This is the water, gold as wine,
of the river whispering rosaries
that feeds the roots of the tiptoe trees
supporting lofty canopies
that shade the chapel where nature prays.

And these are the cloisters in washed-out roots
where church-mice wrens can meditate
on insect-game and nesting-site
or chant Hail Maries, lost in light,
high in the perpendicular choir
of the church where nature prays.

And this is the secular farmer's field
where tractors mow the embroidered grass
of midsummer's vestments, and swallows, filled
with insects bred in the meadow's hide,
go sip the river of holy wine
or chase in the airy chapel's cage
through broken windows of foliage.

And these are the votive candles, set
on the shadowy floor, giving flame-blue light
from luminous flowers along the route
of the river of heavenly reveries
where bluecoat swallows skim deep trout-pools

and – twittering like a Sunday-school
in navy jackets with earwig tails –
they perch in rows along altar rails.

And seed is the answer to nature's prayer:
full as a bible with holy words
to spell out buds and fledgeling birds
and luminous campaniles of flower
spread by autumn's replenishing floods
that furnish the sacred riverside grove –
choir, clerestory, aisle and nave –
with incense, anthem and altar fire
for the church where nature prays.

But where is the builder, Jack-in-the-Green?
He dies in winter to rise in spring
and haunt live pillars whose leafy crowns
mask shining eyes that watch unseen
the visiting swallow and resident wren
and lonely riverside walking man
who senses the gaze of unblinking Jack
conning his tattered and torn heart's book,
and the burden that bows his back
in the church where nature prays.

Vernon Scannell

The Journey: A Dialogue

What preparations did you have to make
for the journey that you chose to undertake?

Not many and quite simple: lots of plain
or lined A4, warm drinks that don't contain
soporific substances, and then,
of course, a pencil or some kind of pen –
whichever is the easier to use
thick blinds for blotting out distracting views,
stout doors for solitude and quietness,
and any kind of comfortable dress.

Did you travel with a dragoman or friend
to offer help and guidance or extend
that welcome word of reassurance when
you might have missed the company of men?

I went alone, of course, as everyone
who's been on such a journey must have done.

And did your journey work out as you'd planned
or was there snow where you expected sand?
To put it simply, did you lose your way,
or get waylaid, or somehow led astray
by sinuous temptations? Did you keep
steady on your course or fall asleep
when senses should have been alert and clear?
Did resolution fade, then disappear?

All of those, and none.

What do you mean?

I mean that, yes, I sometimes found I'd been
led by ignis fatuus or plain
laziness down tracks to bleak terrain
that yielded nothing valuable to me.
But you must understand: there could not be
a plan or chart from which to deviate:
the senses were my compass; vade-mecum, fate.

And did you succeed? How did your journey end?

I found I was unable to contend
with all the twists and obstacles I met
on that long trek. I lost a lot of sweat
for no reward. I didn't ever
find an epiphanic goal of any kind.

What is it like, this place you tried to reach?
A glittering city? Solitary beach
with whispering wavelets fingering the sand?
A place of magic, kind of fairyland?
Primeval woods where innocent killers dwell?

I'll say it once again, so listen well:
I didn't reach it, so how am I to tell?

Fred Beake

Good Men Are Gone Into Another Kingdom

Good men are gone into another kingdom, or into nothing

To something at least that is not themselves

And I am so angry at the cold indifference of death
That the water of my grief is ice
And the flesh of the living is like pictures that pass.

Sebastian Barker

Linger Awhile

Linger a while. Tell me about the news.
Don't go just yet. I tinkered with the clock.
Pull up your chair again. Don't think it mean
To pinch an hour from me, your special friend.

Time snips the corners, whittling down
What little time we have to less than none.
Linger a while. Tell me about your son
Who grew to be a master of the world.

Don't go. The berry leaves are green.
The milk is fresh. And like a Chinese satin screen
My life comes back to me, and with it, yours.
Don't go. The berry leaves are ours.

Hours and hours. The future has a price.
A Jeroboam of wine ought to pay the bill.
The sun is tilting on the melting ice,
And on the table-top your hand is still.

Dana Gioia

Nocturne

(Count Orlock's aria from NOSFERATU*)*

I am the image that darkens your glass,
The shadow that falls wherever you pass,
I am the dream you cannot forget.
The face you remember without having met.

I am the truth that must not be spoken,
The midnight vow that cannot be broken.
I am the bell that tolls out the hours.
I am the fire that warms and devours.

I am the hunger that you have denied
The ache of desire piercing your side.
I am the sin you have never confessed,
The forbidden hand caressing your breast.

You've heard me inside you speak in your dreams,
Sigh in the ocean, whisper in streams.
I am the future you crave and you fear.
You know what I bring. Now I am here.

Terence Reid

In Denial

When we were young and starry-eyed,
brimful of energy,
we hailed the bold, despised the weak,
derided frailty.

We worked hard, played hard, marched as one,
each blue-eyed, fair-haired boy.
Our inspiration, national pride,
our mantra, strength through joy.

And from boyhood through to manhood
we forged an iron will.
Untouched by doubt, we each remained
idealistic still.

We steeled our minds, controlled our hearts,
deaf to cries of terror.
We dressed ourselves in righteousness,
left no room for error.

With half the world against us,
to lose was no disgrace.
We took revenge on lesser breeds;
We're still the master race.

You ask me now, when I am old,
am I beset by shame?
For me, I answer, duty done
exonerates all blame.

I still relive with heady thrill,
despite what's come to pass,
the night we made a fire of books,
the night we splintered glass.

Ian Caws

Wharfs

The ships don't come now. Only rain and weeds
Through the concrete. One evening, we watched
From a boat on the river how light matched
Colours on broken windows and water,
And commented how all the gates and sheds
Were open as if it didn't matter.

Now they are selling the wharfs and we walk
On dry ground. Men in skilled trades and hard hats
Put down their instruments and scribble notes.
Yes, no doubt it is a bad part of town
And we should welcome the rich and their ilk.
Anyway, the ships that came here have gone.

The tides, of course, may still rise in autumn
But it will not be a place for fighting
Or drunkenness. The future, kept waiting,
May leave for good. From windows in the new
Apartments, they will point out, at sea, some
Passing vessel but the ships don't come now.

The watermen will grow old and stroll by
The new gates, see light on modern windows.
And there will be photographs of the days
When the ships came. But we, who are able,
Will walk to the wharfs one last time today,
Catch weather and pull weeds from the rubble.

Richard O'Connell
Murderess

On the morning of her release
after years in jail,
gaunt and coughing
she sat with women guards,
biographer and daughter
– gypsy dressed, theatrical
head band, earrings glittering,
holding court and sway
in an Oxford B & B
while the officious red faced owner
buzzed about her table bringing toast
cut into 'soldiers'
to please the little girl
that somehow still lurked beneath
her pallor and sharp smile.

Maggie Bevan
Candle

Consumed by a need
to shrug free of form,
I must burn ...
my body melts and I,
anorexic, white angel,
start my ascension.

Flesh dissolves –
the world falls away
imperfect as memory;
greedy as boys
all earthly desires strip off –
slip to my feet:
vain dresses;
the lies of mirrors, of eyes,
cloud – go up in smoke
like wisps of smiles,
unvoiced cries ...

Not thin enough yet
I must disappear.
Hungry for absence,
I eat only air,
don't scream
as buttocks, breasts, flatten out
to wax doll innocence –
I want to be sexless
not even a virginal girl.

In control of the future at last
I've found my purpose:
the one thing I excel at.
Don't pity!

This is not hell.
The flame at my head is an eye:
it lights a passage to heaven
as I push back thick dark,
its cloying hands of love
reach up through my halo –
become all mind, pure spirit.

Illuminating the perfect,
I can do anything.
Could even stop if I wanted.
But flame and wax are desperate:
insatiable lovers,
they need each other so much.
Now the fuse is lit there's no going back –
true to its fate
my body goes on
doing away with itself.

I leave it to earth –
see it down there:
just a useless sprawl.
Disgusting flesh
is nothing to do with me.
For I have an x-ray vision.
I have bones in mind:
hard elemental weapons
uncarve –
and soon I won't be touched,
ever,
will be
too flat and aloof to have babies –
but that's just as well
for a woman of wax
would bear only dolls
doomed to smoulder in silence.
To give, like candles.

Gary Allen

Languages

And this is your first real sense of freedom,
flying down the Alp passes on your Norton into Italy
the flight-jacket zipped tight against the wind –
those late-night letters becoming harder to scribble
knowing how heavy every word became in their hands.

The virtues of a good-upbringing and self-respect
that your father tried to impart on that last walk along Tremadog Bay,
as you stared at the creased skin on his face and neck
tattooed blue by years at the coal-face,
are the very things you hurled your youth against
in the bars and brothels of post-war Berlin.

Visits back to the terraced house in Porthmadog becoming rarer
your dress-uniform making you awkward among friends
how you itched to get overseas again
away from uncles, aunts, the solemn chapel Sundays
the rain falling off slates, shop-signs, doorways
like the haemorrhaging hours of childhood –
tracing routes along the marble fireplace.

And you could never understand how a man who spent his life in
                                                     mines
could waste hours studying the texts of your old school grammars –
what Welsh you had flattened out to control-tower monotone
as you talked down combat aircraft over German skies.

His shape still living in the old coat hanging behind the bedroom
                                                     door,
photographs of himself outside pits in the Rhondda during the forties
scattered with pictures of you on the dresser,
and all the postcards you forgot sending while on leave across Europe.

John Greening
1954 –
(FOR S.H.)

Born in a present, peace-torn, eyes
turned to the stinging wake of war,
we are not a generation to take risks.

We were the pill-celebrants, the crash-
barrier, helmet and seat-belt invokers,
spawners of the circuit-breaker, the child lock.

Our parents spoke briefly, through their smoke,
of sleeping in the tube, of counting doodlebugs
to singsongs or shuddering silent withdrawal:

of how they'd had to be evacuated to cold
strangers in cold outbuildings, or were called
up early from their teens to be sent to Iceland.

Our generation stayed at home, were never
head-hunted, could not upgrade or network.
We expected our parents to remain married

so we could tune in weekly to Uncle Mac,
the bomb-sites nursing storeys, the shelters
floral clocks, dumb sirens keeling –

and we'd put up with the Tridents overhead
and the traffic growing heavier on the Great West.
Our parents slept like Hrothgar's men, along

the dark hall, expecting at any
missile crisis or with the next flashed
assassination, the shadow to take hold

and that old hypnotic dangerous spark
centre screen to ignite. We slept through,
except for the first instalment of Dr. Who

or for that giant moon-leap. We dreamt
of risks, of bare skin, and dark
cis-lunar passageways. The ballistics

were all tipped with sex. The bodies
in our heaven were lifeless, though not dead.
Even Aberfan left us untouched.

But our parents watched it all like miners'
faces on a negative. They saw the mountain
moving that we had been made to climb

with them last holiday, hacking for blue,
and scree-running back to see the Mitchell
Minstrels and Dai... Peace grew

noisy, grew problematic. It shifted. It
slid into Indo-Chinese ideograms
and Anglo-Irish graffiti. It smothered

childhood in this dull fear. And still
our parents charge their brittle and corroded
feet to meet these forty years on

head on. What we had so good
has levelled to a lottery. We risk a flutter
that becomes a palpitation, an attack. And ends

in a rollover dream of getting better.

Penelope Shuttle

In all Weathers

A dream cannot procure you
wealth in the world

but it has a gilt-edged tongue,
is an arguer of luminous cunning,

shares out its riches
like any friend sharing sorrows
in all weathers.

Gary Bills

The Older World

The autumn's here, and England starts to rust,
And cidered voices gather in the lane
To fix the price of grain, the fate of sheep,
Before bad weather chases to the hearth
The farmer and his scowl to end the year;
His gun is on the wall, his boots by the chair;
The dog's asleep and will not hear his name.

The autumn's here; the blackberries have burst;
And oak trees huddled close about the church
Release their rooks in gales to swarming skies,
And fields around, once filled with busy ghosts
Who worked beside the combine with the scythe,
Are stubble now, picked over by the crow,
All patient for the gliding touch of flame.

Michael Webb

Cargoes

(for the 1990's after John Masefield)

Quick-freeze trailer-truck, backing to the landing-bay,
loaded with pallets for the Safeway store,
and a cargo of bar-codes
freebies, packaging,
Today's Special Offer! and Savings Galore!

Stately Spanish Tri-star, its wing-tips blinking,
dipping in to land from the Costa del Sol,
with a cargo of pensioners,
memories, suntan,
and crushed malaguena matador dolls.

Dirty British tanker, its radar-dish twirling,
butting up the Channel past the South Coast resorts,
with a cargo of over-drive,
tail-back, pile-up,
body-bags, brain scans and coroners' reports.

Eve Kimber
Wild Child

'He won't sit still'
the teacher said

As a star flickers and palpitates
as a leaf dances in the wind
as a lamb gambols and leaps in the chill February

> As a star flickers and palpitates as it hangs over the void
> as a leaf dances before the wind whirls it forever away
> as a lamb gambols and leaps in the chill February
> > and the fox waits
> > and the wind cuts to the bone
> > and this night lambs will die

As a star flickers and palpitates hanging over the void, a pulse of
joy
as a leaf dances before it flees, as leaves dance ever,
as a lamb leaps in the brief playtime of the year

so my wild child
won't sit still.

Spin the ropes to tie him down,
spin the bonds of stern reproach,
twist the nerves with ordered rows
of children wound in custom's threads.

'All the others can sit still,
listen to the teacher's voice,
learn their lesson, write in tidy lines.'

Pin him down with a label through his heart,
something-lexia, something-phraxia.
O that so old and wise and wild language as Greek
should be corrupted to such purposes!

Spin the ropes to tie him down,
spin the bonds of stern reproach,
twist the nerves with ordered rows
of children wound in custom's threads.

Train him to listen to the teacher
not to the pulses of his own blood
or to the birds outside the window
crying: 'Play in the long grass, beloved of the sun,
where the grasshoppers play all summer;
play in the dark, crowded woods,
among dust and leaves and woodmice;
play on the river's edge, where ducks dabble;
the world and the world's sweetness, and you part of it!'

Spin the ropes to tie him down,
spin the bonds of stern reproach,
twist the nerves with ordered rows
of children wound in custom's threads.

Grow deaf to the words of your blood,
my wild child.
Forget the sweet world and your intemperate joy.
Turn from the silent blaze of the stars and do your homework.
Leave off playing with music and practise your scales.
If they can change you they'll praise you;
print you out a certificate;

but I shall weep for my wild child,
who listened to the song of his blood
and the bird at the window
whose eyes dreamed
whose face was fresh as flowers
and who, like the stars and the leaves and the spring lambs
couldn't sit still.

Tony Turner

Where was I?

In the bathroom. Just thinking
of what I'm doing, but I drift off,
remember something I ought to have done
yesterday, wonder if I can remember
till I get downstairs, write it down.

Or should I stop what I'm doing now
go downstairs and make a note of it?

If I were to pop off now, would that be
the end of it? Light one minute,
dark the next and nothing after?
Where's the soap?

Where's the evidence? It's a dangerous game:
unlimited numbers, objectives unknown,
rules undeclared. Where's the referee?
Fouls happen all the time.
Good luck and bad abound
and the film can never be rewound,
mistakes taken out.

                And yet ... how did bodies
develop defences against germs?
By chance? It looks mighty like design.
Where did I put the toothpaste?

I bet I put it in the cupboard
though I know it's not kept there. No.
Under the flannels?
In the laundry basket! Whatever
was I thinking about?

Did the eagle muse, "I need a talon
so I'll make one. There."?
I don't think so. Darwin would say
some birds had sharper claws
so became meat-eaters.
Perhaps. Did they convert
digestive systems overnight?
So many questions.

No time to get all the answers.
In the end, it's a matter of what
you believe. Where's the toothpaste
top? What a mess. Wipe it up.
Move on. Move on to something else.

Where was I?

June English
Cold October
(for Jan)

Off stage, enjoying wine, two lovers sit.
Although they've heard the bell for curtain call,
They steal a second more and polish it,
Then rise to play their part and give their all.

Sauntering down Place de la Concorde,
A dream they've shared through all their married years
He buys her things she knows he can't afford,
Her love for him holds back the ready tears.

He hides his tiredness by talk, but she
Sees all: the dragging feet that strive and climb;
The way he holds her hand so tenderly,
Then softly lets it slide. How brief is time.

The script's all wrong, but who's to tell? Or know
They laugh when they should cry? She plays her part,
Until the final act when he must go,
Then finds the words burst out from her full heart.

The bitter sweetness of those final days
Distilled by her; by him forever lost,
Embalms the memories she now replays
As cold October turns to winter frost.

Robert Greacen

Twentieth Century Captain Fox

I was wrong. Absolutely wrong.
Carrington-Smythe was wrong.
All who knew Fox were wrong.
We did not know him well enough.
He was the classic Englishman,
Well-spoken, modest, tolerant,
Who always knew the Test Match score.
His bright intellect dimmed slightly
To match his cronies at the Club.
Yet one or two of us could sense
A distance, a hidden tension.
Why did he read Kafka, Rilke,
Listen to Mozart and Alban Berg,
Try his hand at philosophic comment?
'An English eccentric,' said Carrington-Smythe
As he sipped cognac on a Suffolk lawn.
Now the cat has jumped from Hubermann's bag,
His biography a continent of facts,
A mausoleum for the Captain.
Both Fox's parents Jews?
Both victims of the Holocaust?
Young Fox surviving through the Kindertransport?
We were dubious, we laughed it off.
That Swiss Professor must be daft!
But Hubermann has proved his case
With thirty pages of footnotes,
Documents, eye-witness reports.
Bankers' Zürich has unveiled the truth,
The tragic, the prosaic truth,
The provincial banality of evil.
How wrong we were, how un-seeing.
Fox now stands forth as hero, anti-hero,
A self-invented twentieth century man
Whose business was never my business.

Robert Hamberger
Die Bravely

'Why this would make a man a man of salt,
To use his eyes for garden water-pots,
Ay, and laying autumn's dust. I will die bravely,
Like a smug bridegroom.'

'King Lear' (Act 4 Sc.6)

Morning After

Last night we threw all the junk overboard:
chucked out summer photos and simple promises,
their noise fat stones hitting water.
Last night we climbed into our life-rafts
like separate beds.
This morning
the marriage is floating away from us.
If we stretch we can still touch its rudder,
its soaked wood.
Our hands are full enough, steadying ourselves in the wake
where there's no sound of gulls, no sight of land,
only sea growing flatter between us in a new light.

Your First Words

"Can I say hello to you?" We were eighteen
first night away from home, and I said yes.
You thought I looked safe. How could you guess
in years to come I'd sometimes leave the room when
you were talking, annul you like that, how often
I'd stone you with silence. If I managed to impress
that night with quotes from Plath it didn't take us
long to learn no-one lives by poetry alone.
Pillow-talk on student grants. Two virgins touching

skin and histories. Speech ran
its thread down boulevards and cul-de-sacs, finding
all there is to know about one person.
Twenty years on I barely know you, but thanks for asking.
Go back to that night and I'd say yes again.

Separation Suite

They sit a chair apart,
move when the counsellor calls them
to a room where they're meant to relate.
Three fawn chairs and they talk about needs.
She's only starting to imagine hers,
can't begin to name them. He's written a list.
Next week he's back without her.
One voice slumped against magnolia woodchip:
his pain aria, his monotonous solo.

Looking At Wedding Photos

Who are these kids dressed as adults, thinking
they can throw a promise at the future
and it won't shatter after sixteen years? They're
sticking a knife in the cake hand over hand, grinning
fit to burst. Remember that Just Married sign
felt-tipped on the back of a Rat Poison container,
your dad getting lost, yellow roses, our
first married row on the wedding
night round Salisbury's one-way system. All gone.
What happened next? Happiness. Mistakes. Slowly seeing
                                                we've
got to cut our losses. I won't burn
these smiles. They're proof of love,
while our children who never existed then
hold out their gifts: three reasons to survive.

The Old Words

While my hands soak up to their wrists in water
and the kids breathe asleep upstairs
my head's a hive with you and him naked in it.
Funny how the old words come back.
Fuck. Adultery. Cuckold. Betrayal.
I want this porn-film out of my hair:
to wash off what your body's doing, not doing
your skin a map I can no longer follow,
whetstone where a new knife twists.

Ivy House

A couple of dreamers. We'd make our ideal home.
So what if the owners were splitting up?
We were rock solid, seduced by each snowdrop
daffodil and door-frame, the view from every room.
We put down roots: damp-proofed, re-wired, sprayed
                                        woodworm,
coated on buckets of gloss. We couldn't stop
until french windows had their cat-flap
and kids' hand-marks swiped the walls. It was high time
to look at what we'd done. I stayed tense
as barbed wire while you started scratching
a tunnel out. The builder said subsidence:
that quarter-inch crack down the north wall. Re-pointing
can't cure it. A fine romance.
It'll cost an arm and a leg now the drains are collapsing.

From Under The Shadow

Don't kid yourself it's easy.
My shadow's not as vacuous as air,
some sticky web wiped from footsoles.
It's heavy as a man's body on you
squeezing out your breath.
We pressed grids across each other,

tattooing a street-plan of bruises
under our skin: husband father wife mother.
Live in my image. We couldn't fit.
Rip the maps,
learn our names again, recognize for the first time
your face, my face at noon where nettle paths divide
and our shadows shrink to puddles we step over.

Slow Learner

I keep rehearsing the call you won't make
one night near midnight in a few months: "I was wrong.
He's nothing to me. I've loved you all along.
I see things now. I made a mistake.
We both did, but we've learnt from it. If we take
our time maybe we could look at starting again." This daft
                                                        song
round my skull, these phrases that don't belong
in your mouth but in mine, or that fake
image I still have of you. I never could see
what was an inch from my nose. It's like two days
before Clifford died, when they'd already
upped the morphine, his doctor friend says
"You know he's dying don't you?" I thought he can't be.
He'll recover. Pinning my hopes on another bad phrase.

Talk Before Bedtime

Our son touches his forehead
runs a hand down his body to his feet:
"I felt sad from here to here."

We talk about sadness
how you and I can't make each other happy.

Squeezing my ribs in his tightest bear-hug
he laughs and asks "Does that hurt?"

In Front Of The Kids

When I cried in front of the kids they asked why.
"I've made you unhappy." That was enough.
I didn't add no-one would choose this rough
ride for their children, how I followed my
father's footsteps by walking out. That advert family
drops through the floorboards. I won't bluff
my way through failing as husband or father. My tough
son ran for toilet-paper to dry
my eyes. He said "I want to see you"
and gently held my face between his hands.
If this home's broken we'll build something new
from the four times a week when I'm with them, stroking
                                        strands
of hair off their hot brows. We slip through
absences, over stones, and our river never ends.

Benediction

Bless you for entering through a door-crack
and opening windows. For three children.
Without them my life would be one room,
books and a bare lightbulb, a locked cupboard.

For knowing when we needed to end:
saving us years of petty victories
over dinner, on a drive, our children
watching and hearing, a gagged audience.

For handing me back to myself:
giving up your responsibility, saying
"He's yours now. Make of his life what you can."

Truce

Call a truce. I'll bite my tongue and remember
how your breath fanned my back while we slept.
If it tickled my skin I shifted, slipped

an arm around your waist sometimes, or under
the duvet on good nights you squeezed my shoulder.
No need for talking in our sleep. Our bodies kept
their independent language, whose tides swept
us up pebbles and rolled us down. Until the past year
made us kneel yards apart on a hard coast.
Six weeks after we faced that truth
it was almost the old days. You dozed on my chest
as if you were my wife again, my breath
against your hair. Letting go. The last time we kissed
I lightly nipped your tongue between my teeth.

Her Voice

I haven't walked far enough. I can still hear it:
her words repeat in my head
until they're mine.

Hedges creak in the wind like bed-springs.
Her voice will go the way of rain:
shrink to a shallowing puddle, dry in the sun.

I can sit it out
while that noise from one skylark in the next field
flickers its singed coal above my breathing.

Rose Flint

Women Making Bridges Out Of Nets

We have a part in building each other's bridges
over this next river. Our words feeling out
these shaky structures, their delicacy and strength,
the naked places where we need a spar to shore us up,
a warm touch to earth us through these uncertain months
of storm and fire. Gifts we give go soul to soul,
make us real, even in these new unwieldy bags
of aging skin.

> *Gifts of beaded parrot feathers*
> *blue as tomorrow's magic wing.*
> *Angel cake at Lammas. The wine*
> *you didn't drink alone. A red silk shirt*
> *so wintery, and bright*
> *as any blood.*

We all cry the river.
Sometimes it seems we only swim upstream
like salmon homing in to die
we struggle, leap impossibilities;
somehow get past our children's traumas,
our mirror's fickle alterations, our cloudy loves.
Sometimes we flow like drowned fish-wives,
slide down to the ocean with only our mouths faint sigh
above the dreaming wave.
But one of us will call, throw out a lifeline.
In sunset kitchens where adult daughters
glide like strangers or come and go, breathless
as shooting stars trailed with quickly fading light
we talk the dark; place the knots and threads
of our own experience; remind each other
that salmon are considered wise.

Others crossed before we came, left signs and stories,
coded metaphors of witches and their transformations.
We leave gardens, rituals, recipes – faint ghosts
of our bridges in silver lines fine as flying hair.
Our daughters may understand, and follow
– but each day the way is newly made.

It's a round dance and we touch fingertip to tip
as we spin towards our separate, secret destinations.

Mimi Khalvati

River Sonnet

Welling up in her fingers, water runnelled
seaward through stones. She wasn't watching water.
Or thinking of tomorrow — how time funnelled,
flows. Water was doing her thinking for her.
Draining down her thoughts till they ran as lightly
as leaves across a playground, rose to torment
branches that had borne them, betrayed them, nightly
blurred distinctions, daily held to their bent
and finally torn loose. She heard the river
babble, level, contradictions resolve in
a rush, out of her hands, felt quarrels fly
in droves. *Who-o-o* the river sang, *ivbo-so-ever*
clouds rang round the sky, sky thinking itself in
river, river thinking itself in sky.

193

Leah Fritz

Yeats

(i.m., Sylvia Plath)

I hurry past, no longer see the plaque
above the bell in memory of Yeats,
the carapace of sorrow where she sat.
(Each day the green of life is freshly made
just yards away.) She could not shed that shell's
dead weight, but turned the leaden ache to gold,
while children slept. She claimed she did death well;
thought dying proved it. But lead in Fitzroy Road
is lead, not gold. 'Damn near blew up the kids,
the house, the street. Ought to've taken a leaf
from him, up there. Grown old,' a neighbour said,
'listening in Sligo to the bees.'

Danielle Hope

The Alternative History of Jemima Puddle-Duck

So much worse this century than the last
you claim over *canard au gratin* in Camden
Somme, Gallipoli, Blitzkriegn, Belsen.
How eagerly we assent you are right –
    recall Boers, Jews, Muslims who stormed and died
concentrated in camps. Final primitive
forests are razed, whales fail, ice-caps dissolve,
offices tower, tramps clutter the road.

                            It's late, my car
weaves home; rain pebbles the windscreen.
Another wrong turn and lost on route.
Last century my same-aged ancestor
was already dead, in childbirth or rape
fought forgotten wars, cholera, starvation.
No Beatrix Potter values by the kitchen fire.

Jeremy Page

Bathing

As I break the water
with my own version of breaststroke,
my children watch in silence
from the shore and suddenly
everyone whose daily life collides
with mine is not there.

They have taken their baggage
in all its shapes and guises
and retreated up the beach,
till they are hidden by
the parapet of shingle.
The water performs its trick
of going from ice-cold to cool
until it seems the temperature
of the blood coursing through
my veins, and the light mist
that hugs the Channel soothes
and warms my limbs. The sensation
of seaweed round my toes
is unfamiliar these days, but its
coarse dry greenness is welcome,
and these ten minutes when the
hands on my watch are still, when the
silent children on the beach are the
only witnesses, are balm for the soul.

I wade ashore to their gentle applause,
pebbles painful underfoot, and already
there are figures moving, indistinct but
purposeful, down the beach.

Peter Redgrove
The Verdurer

The verdurer records
 the woodsound in his notebook
  to study the tree's pulses
Indoors. As he returns
 he passes under wild pines
  wracked by their anguish
To great size.
 These trees are avatars
  of the books on his shelves,
The foliage blowing open
 blowing shut –
  he knows their titles,
Scotch Pine, Crackwillow,
 Alder,
  and reads their green;
The library is an avatar
 of the forest, with each book
  a haunted corner
Until he closes
 the wooden covers
  'When in such an embrace
Your nerves are shaken as leaves,
 enter this shaking'
  he leaves
This book or forest
 wide open on the wooden table
  for its good advice

Alan Brownjohn
Throwback

Ridiculous no one told them they could stop:
At the extreme end of a corridor
Was the ballroom of a once Grand Hotel,
Sold and left to the weather to close it down.
I could curiously hear as we walked along it
(I and somebody else who might have been
Any one, I suppose, of a number of friends)
Certain amplified sounds, more amplified by echoes,
Turning out to be music. Surely it couldn't be
An orchestra still at it? It could be the wind?

But there, when we walked in over the fallen door
And across the plaster fallen from the ceiling
(As on one night of my early adolescence,
When I followed, at her suggestion, Dolores O'Leary,
Her real name, on VE-night, in Sportsbank Hall
As a flying bomb left it) were a bride and a groom
Still dancing, still dressed in their wedding stuff.
To see them even now, circling round, looking over
Each other's shoulders, didn't seem quite right.
Nor did their calling to me by my real name.

James Brockway

A.D. 2000

Time does not exist of the numbers
we stamp on it, on which we insist:
like 2 oh oh oh. Time's elastic.
The other day I was back in Switzerland
a good thirty years ago, lost
on a lake where time was mist.

Time is a feeling in the air,
time's not really there.
But man, as history shows,
lives by illusion. Time comes and goes.

Alexis Lykiard

Terminal

Shortest day '99. This cherished doctor friend,
by way of cheerful emphasis – he feels all right –
most gladly offers us a twenty-year-old wine.

Our truest toast should wish for a quick, painless end,
yet fears aren't voiced. He speaks of how he plans to spend

the few remaining days before Millennium.
Who'd speculate now on a century to come?

Each glass is drained. And unforced laughter pours a fine
placebo, loving cup to help forget the night ...
His wave seems brave enough, as we move out of sight.

Fred Beake
Song at 51

The sky is grey and has no end.
I can see no mortal building.
Even the sheep are gone away
And no birds give hint of song.

The only music is the wind's
And it pushes at me
As if to overturn and break
Whatever stands in its way.

Soon no doubt I shall be dust
And joyful in the gale.
But today I must keep my feet
And hope my courage is adequate.

First hope and love have ended.
I may see red berries on that bush
Down by that stream we walked along
When we were very young

But I shall see them alone,
And their brightness be of death
And not the first discovery of self
And purpose in this life.

Tread on! Tread on! Most things can change
And this despair will pass.
But from now I walk to another state
I must face without abhorrence.

Robert Greacen

Cartographers

Old men are cartographers.
We map the coloured countries
Our childhood dreamed of.
Down the corridors of years
We see the streets of freedom
Where pirates and cowboys roam;
The tram that clangs to Eden,
The ships heading for exotic ports:
Marseilles, Piraeus, St. Petersburg.
Lands and seas light up
As we lie in the dark,
Hopping from country to country.
Old men before and after sleep
Draw maps, hear distant voices.
River gods and sirens sing us
To islands, deltas, archipelagoes.

Patrick Osada
Twos

Today we did human biology:
Why, she asked, are we made of twos? –
Two arms, two legs, two eyes, two ears.

Struggling with the grand design,
I came up with emergencies –
How we have something in reserve,
Should any one of those go wrong.

Now, thinking of you far away,
I feel that distance play its part;
I puzzle like she did today –
Wondering why, only one heart?

Ken Smith
Evening Primrose

Every moment itself, at dusk the many greens
of the darkening garden, background to the sheer
white sheets of the hydrangea, the yellow cups
St. John's Wort offers to the deepening blue.

The opening of the hour of the evening primrose,
the last homeward chatter of the blackbird,
that moment the city's traffic stills. Music,
perhaps, a little night music on the FM,

Bach's Staccato in B Minor, a little Mozart,
Relax relax natters the DJ, a plane drills
a hole in the horizon, a siren wails its urgent mission,
and the world's with us again. Nag. Nag.

Still, there were moments, yellow flowers
closing in the last of the last light, musk
of lavender and woodruff and a cool breeze
in the long half-light that becomes no light at all.

Rose Flint

Heavy Air

Some days I just stop and want you here beside me
– even though you'll be home in an hour or so
and nothing is wrong – it's a need to charm the Fates
as if I could wear the nearness of love as an amulet.
On these days, if you return unexpectedly
then even light releases its breath.

I don't breathe easy. I'm too aware
of the preciousness of air, its vitality
held in such a fragile vessel as a body.
Such a slight thing – a sigh – to hold a life.

I feel it now, high in the quick shallows,
air sucked in and out so fast I try to compensate,
breathe deeply until everything constricts and I
could drown   *a wave of pale blue tulle*
    ruched and full, perfume – Mother going dancing.
I must have been involved with those little pots of rouge,
white downy powderpuffs. She showed me
the absence of her breasts. Scorched maroon skin's texture
rough and mottled and a hollowness, as if her selfness
had been burned in to the bone.

Sea-whispers rustling between every snowy tissue layer
in the box that held the folded dress. My sudden breasts
terrifying as first blood.

Christmas: blue cedars heavy with snow, sunset
firing the smooth white shadowed garden: stillness.
    When she died, the whirlpool of her breathing
collected every living breath within the house to sough
and rattle, rasp within her branded concave chest

the whole house breathless   and black
filtering under the doors like suffocating ash.

I can't remember her. There's too little, only this
constricting legacy of heavy air around the heart
and this need sometimes, for the simple anchor of your kiss.

Ruth Fainlight
Black

A crow
in the middle of the road
like a brushstroke
marking a word
on an opened scroll
in a script I cannot read

that only lifts
as I approach
at the last moment
with a sudden clap
of wings, abrupt

a messenger
to search me out
on this empty stretch
of country road
with a summons
from the lord of poetry
and prophecy – or
the black god of death.

(earlier version of the poem which later appeared in Burning Wire. *See acknowledgements.)*

June Hall

Snakes

'I'm here to listen,' he says
and smoothes the space between us.
Unlistening he runs
his polished measure over me,
pumps arms, pivots hands,
rotates wrists, commands eye swivels,
beams at the snake spirals he has me draw.
'Better than mine,' he lies.

Content, he offers me his arm,
and offers too his malediction:
'Things will get worse!'
Cleanly he chops through hope
then slivers and slices it dead,
conveys with oiled assurance
how others have imagined improvement
only to be proved wrong
for like a slow-moving escalator
the disease, relentless,
will progress.

I query his catechism of certainty.
His suit grows darker, his smile
wider as it cracks around the mouth.

Snakes point towards me.

A.C. Clarke

Last Glimpse

The last time I saw you, to say I saw you
and not the shell that sickness burned you to
the last time I saw you alone

you were standing at the top of iron stairs
from street level to station concourse
your hair a little wild

You weren't looking in my direction
but into the middle distance
You looked anxious
I had forgotten how small you were

You started when I greeted you

Your eyes were watering and I noticed
the spider veins in your cheek
bunched into scarlet knots

You still walked firmly but there was
a hesitancy there

There was hesitancy later
when you turned to me in the street
asking in a voice not yours 'Where are we?'
and looked at me like a small girl

I could not speak
someone was walking over my grave

Chandani Shah

For Winter

Be the tender sun of a winter's dawning,
gently unfold the mist and open this land to the skies.
Be the noble star that shines in the north, faithful/everlasting,
point out paths and make apparent meanings.

Let your footsteps move ahead, always,
touch every village, barn, lawn, and watering place.
Keep your hopes fervent forever,
remove challenges/obstructions.

Become illumination, full of understanding, increasingly
burning,
light up countless wickers as you move along.
Touch the heartbeat of each and every Nepali
fill love for their nation in their being.

Reach every hill/terrace and field.
Search each line, every space of our land.
Spread melodies of peace throughout this earth,
create a grand history for this country.

Susan Skinner

The Wood

You found the centre of a wood
where no-one goes before their death,
and in a clearing understood
life's dream, the marvel of life's breath.

A bird flew down from leaf to leaf
and sung of silence and release
from love and loss and hope and grief,
and sang of death's undying peace.

You lay beneath the summer trees.
You did not think of why or when.
You only knew you longed for peace
and could not grieve for peace again.

Stella Davis

Coffee in Weimar

Our feast of contradiction.
Glazed and gleaming pastries, such
many-coloured morsels,
such *schokalade*, frothed in gilded cups,
such women, idling at table in shiny shoes,
voices and gestures the negligent
assertions of the self-assured.

Here we sit prepared, ah yes, to marvel,
trickling opalescent stones of sugar
into our coffee, raising a sober toast
to the giant luminaries of the city state,

having walked with them all morning over cobbles,
visited their houses, rubbed our fingers
down the smooth wood of their doorposts, nodded
at each statue as though to an old friend,

for here is Bach, there Schiller,
Goethe is everywhere: such weighted names
to thrust breath from our bodies:
imagine them, and gasp.

We linger. We do not want to move.
We would rather stay here, where life was admirable,
pursuing the splendid, catching at their coatsleeves,
holding their stone cold hands.

But the last drop is drunk, the women
haved tapped their quick heels across the pavement
the warmth of the afternoon is on us.
nothing for it now. We make the drive.

And so short a journey it is, such
a little way, for the first beech
almost before we leave the town
grows at the roadside, slender *buch* in leaf
grasping for light, its branches, twigs
all supplicating fingers,
lifted to beg the reasonable air:
what is it that we are come to? How
could we have come to this?

Quiet under a clear spring sunshine
the tall trunks of the Buchenwald
grope upwards to the sky.

Lotte Kramer

Exodus

For all mothers in anguish
Pushing out their babies
In a small basket

To let the river cradle them
And kind hands find
And nurture them

Providing safety
In a hostile world:
Our constant gratitude.

As in this last century
The crowded trains
Taking us away from home

Became our baby baskets
Rattling to foreign parts
Our exodus from death.

Wanda Barford

Black Thomas

(after a visit to the Imperial War Museum's Holocaust Exhibition)

Thomas the tank engine's face is black.
He's been to hell, to hell and back,
swerving and swaying on a thin narrow track.

His eyes are flames and his mouth is red.
In the wagon there's straw, wet straw for a bed;
but no cattle or sheep, just people instead.

As he reaches the gate there's a distant bell,
but no sound is heard, not a shout or a yell.
They've all gone quiet with the silence of hell.

And he puffs with a smoke that's yellowy black
to match that column up there at the back
that's rising and rising from a chimney-stack.

And when he's delivered these women and men
he goes back for more, again and again,
again and again, and again and again.

Stuart Flynn

Just Another Day in a Poet's Study

I sat down to write about what happened to me today;
in times like these there can be no better subject.
Cupid appeared, naked as always, holding
his bow and arrows. "Well, hello," I said,
"I think it's the house next door you want."

"No," said the boy, resting his bow on a pile
of rejection slips, "I am here to inspire you
to write about love." "I would like to be able to oblige,"
I replied, "but that can't be done any more,
and besides, I have no one suitable to write about.

Now, if you will excuse me, I must write about myself.
In times like these there can be no better subject."
The young exhibitionist vanished, and I returned
to thinking of a theme, when my vacant thoughts
were interrupted by slow steps upon the stairs

followed by a knock at the door. Standing outside
was an old blind man with a long white beard. "I'm sorry,"
                                                          I said
"but I am only a poor poet (in both senses of the word),
and I have nothing to give." "I am Homer," he said,
"come to tell you to write of battles, ravishment

and the gods' love affairs." I thought for a moment.
"I don't think anything like that has happened around here
for a while, but ask next door just the same." He shuffled
                                                          away,

while I racked my brains for something of today;
in times like these there can be no better subject.
The telephone rang just before lunch. "Dante here,"
said a voice at the other end, "I am moving between circles

at the moment, so my mobile might cut out suddenly."
"How may I help you?" I asked, wanting to get back to
                                                    my poem
of everyday life. "Have you ever thought," he began,
                                                    "of writing

an epic of the soul's progress from sin to sanctity?"
"Not recently," I replied, "and to be perfectly honest,
in times like these –"   "Yes, I heard you before," he said and
                                                    hung up.
With all those pauses I have not written a poem on today;
and as we know, in times like these, there can be
                        no better subject.

Sheenagh Pugh

Beware of the Elderly

(Road sign in Powys)

It isn't just the stick slid artlessly
out to trip you; it isn't just the wheelchair

over the foot. Nor the tea they make you
in the unwashed cup, its cracks swarming.

It isn't even the hardening opinions,
the way quite sane-looking grandmothers

suddenly hit you with poisoned darts
from the Daily Mail: lorryloads

of gay Rumanian gypsy asylum-seekers
taking time off drug-dealing to get married.

What you really have to watch out for
is the gratitude when you call round

now and then, the long monologues
while your eyes stray to the clock. The guilt

they slip under your guard, the way
their faces ambush you with a look

you've seen in the mirror on bad mornings
and will see on good ones, soon enough.

Caroline Carver

LifeCycle

...clever people
grew out of the earth
or perhaps they came from the comet

they hunted animals in the pastures
fish in the sea
planted crops in the rich soil

and took metals from the rocks
made weapons and tools
built houses on the land
and ships for the oceans

and when they had covered the world with people
there were many who had little
living by the land and its rules

but others who became selfish
and prospered
and took more and more
and replaced less and less

until the world did not have

enough food to eat   enough water to drink
enough fuel for warmth

and the men took up weapons
fought terrible battles
destroyed all the cities
burned all the people

until more
clever people
grew out of the earth
or perhaps they came from the comet ...

Michael Bartholomew-Biggs

Their Minds were Settled

Their minds were settled as they went on board
with one-way tickets – more than they would need.
Six dozen virgins each seemed fair reward.

One purpose bound them tightly like a cord.
With wooden faces no-one else could read
their minds were settled as they went on board

believing that the heavens would applaud
their private holy war surprise attack.
Six dozen virgins each seemed fair reward.

Fierce obsession easily ignored
the screams of panic. They would not turn back:
their minds were settled as they went on board.

And all were dead as burning petrol poured
through buildings folding under their own weight.
Six dozen virgins each seemed fair reward.

Those undetected stanley-knives have scored
the calendar, that unsuspecting date.
Six dozen virgins each seemed fair reward:
their minds were settled as they went on board.

Rupert M. Loydell

In Real Time

Such beautiful images
with the volume down:
slow motion fireballs,
dust fountains, towers
collapsing in the sun;
replay after replay.

Under the wreckage
where the bodies lie
mobile telephones ring,
needing answers and
wanting the truth
about life and death.

Soldiers and reporters
seek answers in black boxes.
I cannot understand
the dark heart of man,
or see through the smoke
of violence and loss.

A plane is flying
across the screen,
a prayer is rising
through my tears:
lead us from ruin
into light.

W.N. Herbert

That the Towers Fell like Troy

'None of us was there to see the siege of Troy,
the fall of Constantinople, the burning of Rome,
the Great Fire of London' — Blake Morrison

Troy was a small town —
we think too big now.
A few thousand looked
at massacre, not a book.

And yet its heroes
survive the sack of years,
their moods and mothers
and the moment of their deaths.

Small towns know grief's grip
and Troy did not escape:
each death was family,
the city shrank to a home.

It was lost the way we lose
our own, who are not called heroes.

Ken Smith

Just one of you

Sarah, while you were at your keyboard,
online to Japan, on the phone to your boyfriend,
just opening your inbox, scratching your ear,
playing Solitaire while you thought no one was looking,

Flight 175 was homing in on you and all those
you'd shared lunch with, a glass of white wine,
secrets you shared with not many. Ground zero
they call it now. And you, you're in the long queue to heaven.

When you were in diapers he was in his mother,
his father on some road to Damascus, the desert
sparks flying in his eyes. You were in kindergarten,
he was forming the first words of his language.

He was fluent then, when you were in grade school,
high school, college, he was learning by heart
his holy book, by the time you were no longer a virgin
he knew the insides and outsides of Kalashnikovs,

M16s, hand helds. He had a licence to fly. There was a plan.
While it was forming you were on vacation in Florida
You were phoning your mother, getting drunk
for the first time. And so perhaps was he.

Your assassin, who flew in from Boston
on an unscheduled flight, smack into you,
your keyboard, your modem, your coffee,
everyone you loved. Like a huge terrible kiss.

Edward Storey

Between Two days

A girl sat dreaming at her desk
and, through the classroom window, saw
a vapour trail chalked on the morning sky.

> *Now don't forget*, she heard the teacher say,
> *to write the title on page one*
> *together with your name and then the date.*

"I know someone up there," she thought,
and smiled to hear her mother's plea –
"Don't cry. I shan't be long. It's only for a day."

> (All distances are short when flights
> out-pace the sun, and offices can be
> just hours away in London or New York.)

"Tomorrow, she'll return, that's what
the days now mean to me. I'll
write the date in when I know she's back."

> But other planes were menacing the sky
> on missions that would contradict
> all pre-arrangements and reunions.

No history book has ever told before
how suddenly so many died
for one fanatic's suicide.

> *Now yesterday*, the teacher said ...
> But that same girl was still not listening.
> The vapour trail had now become a scar.

"I knew someone up there the day before
and I am trying now, Miss, not to cry.
My mother would not want that, but it's hard

to realize between two days
she vanished into fire, dust and air,
and won't come home which ever date I write."

Elizabeth Smither

Rainbow

It appears, it is there, like something
emanating from an emotional source
or a complicated chemical reaction:

here are the colours, red, orange, yellow ...
just now fixed: the sky is the developing tank
and the promise hangs there, suspended

by invisible pegs. It will not stay long:
the coming into being, the becoming
if anyone notices it, fortuitously, its message

is to take from it whatever significance
seems appropriate: a promise with a
time-frame, a statute of limitations.

Dinah Livingstone
October 2001

War came. Bombs fell again.
Poor people tried to flee,
clutching their ragged children,
towards winter without food.
They throng my eyes and mind
with helpless responsibility.
Fear of attack on London.
My dearest, beware the tube,
the fireball, seeping poison.

Meanwhile, on Hampstead Heath,
an autumn spurt of growth,
fresh brilliance in the grass
from spongy turf, my step more
elastic in the noble presence of trees,
each shape quintessentially distinct,
full dressed in waving leaves
becoming radiant before they fall.
Life's sweetness aches the urgency of peace.

Geoffrey Godbert

The Traveller

In memory of Howard Fry

I can tell you this, that when
he died the entirely expected
happened: flowers continued to bloom,
the sun to shine and the moon to rise
as if on a heavenly sigh
of the spirit of him waking
from what had been his silence.

What was totally unexpected
were the sharp breezes of his memory
rustling exotic labels
marking the travels of his life,
stirring his empty luggage
with the names of places he could
visit again at will; and one
he would see for the very first time.

Keith McFarlane

Dunblane

i.m. Lillian Lamb McCall, 1903 – 1997

When they said: Dunblane, Perthshire; I heard
only my childhood: shopping with Nana
and breakfast in bed, eating fish and chips
at the 'talies; walking on heather past
the sound of a burn; criss-crossing sheep-tracks,
on hill-land and moor-land perfumed like honey;
summers spent dreaming in whispering grass.

Once when the snow of the year lay down
in silence, we waded through drifts
to a pine-forest clearing, found there a hind
who was rooting for lichens, hooves and mouth
rasping the once living stems.

                    Now I hear
gunfire and the crying of children;
the sky broken over with ramparts of cloud;
I am back in the Cathedral: thundering
Sundays; stones earthing sky. In the remembrance
of my childhood I see twenty flowers,
white as the snowdrops: the ground
                        is stained red.

On March 13th 1996, at Dunblane Primary School, Thomas Hamilton shot dead seventeen children and their teacher; a further ten children and three teachers were wounded. Having fired 105 rounds in a space of three or four minutes, Hamilton then killed himself with a single shot to the head.

Maggie Butt

Spaces

Huge crimson doors flung wide
shameless as a strip-tease
reveal a cavernous space
empty of fire engines,
and four black lace-up shoes tossed
higgledy-piggledy on the concrete
smelling of socks and haste.
Shouts and running tremble
to silence in the exhaled air.

So it must be in war-time when
young pilots scramble to the skies
leaving half-drunk tea, a bitten sandwich,
a hanger, ballroom-vast and lofty,
echoing with the age-old
adrenaline of going into battle.

But there are greater spaces still
recently vacated, large as light
palpable and noisome
wind eddying in the rafters,
and clues to read them:
spectacles sightless on the hall table
a book, face down, wordless, by the bed.

Sally Carr
Red Silk

Kabul, Kandahar, Kate Adie, Karam.
Terrain, targets, Tornadoes, Tomahawks.
A storm of suicide attacks ... seismic events.

Today, nine pages in *The Guardian*, ten
The Telegraph, ten *The Independent*.
A twenty-four-hour comment bombardment.

The Global Village: but not as McLuhan
had envisaged. Homes secretly tuned
to the World Service each evening;

Al Jazeera beamed to Algeria,
Indonesia; the face that launched
a thousand warheads, a thousand alarms.

Yet women in burqas like winding sheets,
are faceless, unnerving, inscrutable,
diminished ... She writes: My small rebellion

to wear lipstick unseen ... to hide a red silk
party dress from the days of the monarchy ...
Do you play loud music and swim in lakes? ...

Images overload in this unremitting
dream: where the plague bacillus, anthrax
vie with lives burnt to cinders; terror by

mobile phone; stunned politicians; hunger;
alliance diplomacy; deep hatred.
Yet this letter smuggled to Quetta

strikes closest to my news-hardened heart.
She gives a false name, says she could write
pages in her grief, doesn't know where to start.

With acknowledgements.

Judi Benson

Burying the Ancestors

1.

I'm tired of being crooned to the tune
of old Aunt Liza's dead goose,
lullabyed in those cotton fields back home,
roused to Dixie, swamped in the Sewanee River,
hearing Mammy say *hush chile,*
you know your Mamma was born to die.
The one they called Morning, born into the light,
taking her mamma's life. *Hush chile. Hush Mammy.*

I want the repeat names to stop repeating,
all those Henry fathers, greats and grands,
uncles, brothers, cousins intertwined, intermarried.
Juniors, Seniors, and all those Roman numerals, just delete.

Set fire to the tissue-thin letters of fine penmanship
and not much to say, *weather's fine,*
coming home in the covered wagon.
Clip the stamps, give them to the collector,
then burn baby burn.

Burn all their blusterings, their justifications
for blistering others' skin in the relentless summer heat,
while they wrapped themselves around shady porches.

I know to honour this blood flowing through me
is to say nothing. Don't mention the wills
begetting slaves and all their increase, forever, amen.
Sadie, Cicely, Moses, Caesar, and the one they called Patience.
Chains around their necks, chains around their ankles,
chains around their hopeless hearts,
all for the increase of those who refused to work the land,
whose hands were forbidden to touch dirt.

But my tongue wants to be released from its stays.
All those big hats bouncing with flowers, tossed in the wind,
pale faces unveiled, finding a trace of the darker hue hinted at.

II.
Let Eugenia in her ball gown go waltzing
back out the door.   Stop fanning her lashes at the Judge,
begging him to pass the Secession Act on her birthday.
Pretty please Judge, I'll be 19. And so he did,
slicing Georgia off from the Union.

And then what, and what if only Johnny had
come marching home again.
Eugenia, dead of night, bundling her babies
into the flat wagon, crossing the rising river,
just before the bridge gave out,
whipping the horses and cursing those damn Yankees
she'd never forgive, nor all her increase.

Eugenia always seen in mourning-black,
burying her father, her babies, her husband.
Rocking on her porch, silver-haired,
a black ribbon round her neck, glint in her eye,
sure the South would rise again.

III.
Soft people, hard people, lines crissing and crossing
the economic divide, rattling at the edges of china cups,
hands cracked from hard work, soft hands slipping into gloves.
Ladies and Gents, rebels and ruffians.

These strangers: Benjamin, Lydia, Josh and Jasmine,
flattened in the black and white photograph,
sitting stiffly, even when casual,
suspicious of the man under black cloth
the little box with the sudden *Pop!*

Smile. Say cheese. What's that?
Meat? No one's had any in months,
cracked corn, bucked wheat,
and always hoe cake, though once
it was told, syrup.

Once the land was fertile.
Then grew to be like its people, over-worked, exhausted,
tobacco, cotton, corn, thirsty for rain.
The great greats and not-so-greats
with their sharp pulled-back hair,
tight knots, tributaries of trouble
running across their faces,
bending their mouths down,
bones edging through the little skin.
Even the old-eyed children
clench an angry desperation in their faces.

Left-overs, that was all some could afford to rent.
All they had, they'd inherited, the feather bed,
one scrawny mule, three slaves and all their increase.
Just another mouth to feed.

IV.
Planters, plantation owners, preachers, politicians,
doctors, lawyers, artists, teachers, n'er do wells, drunks,
do-gooders, glamour girls posing for Coca Cola ads:
Camille, Vally, Lamar,
naughty girls seen smoking in public, racey women,
swell men, bootleg whisky, speakeasys, suicides,
insanity, vanity and humility. Anecdotes and ancient history,
all it boils down to. Stories told, changed in the telling.

Henry was driving through the back roads in his Model T,
so fast he killed a bunch of chickens on the dusty Georgia clay.

How much? Make it fifteen dollars.
How much? Make it fifteen dollars.
Here's 30, cause I'm coming back just as fast.

Little Henry, Big Henry, dead Henry.

Some lost to sea, some to land. War heroes,
influenza victims, gamblers, ladies' men,
loose women, tight-laced Baptists, Huguenots,
shouting Methodists,
Klan members and Abolitionists,
Suffragettes and Southern Belles,
side by side now, bones mouldering together,
mixing up the arguments, leaving all that love hanging.

V.
They were just people, sugah, father said –
They worked hard and were honest. Religious folk,
never played cards on Sunday, never mixed with coloreds.
Amen. Praise the Lord and pass the ammunition,
pass the succotash, pass the buck, cross yourself,
swear to tell the truth, pray the Lord your soul to take
and all that hate: Absalom, Walter, Kitty, Caroline,
Dolly with the hole in her stocking, dance with her,
dance with all her dead. Jason with the hole in his head, fix
it.
The named and never named, the never talked about one
who ran away with the chauffeur, the older one who stayed,
the one forever missing in action,
the ones whose minds flew away.

VI.
Go away then, I tell them. Stop your whispering in shadows,
plucking at my scalp, sucking at my conscience.
Half-words almost heard,
how my hands are too soft and my thinking too,
how we've all gone soft.

They puzzle over the flushing of the loo.
Wonder why we waste the rich soil
they gave their lives to,
growing flowers that bear no fruit.
Lena, Ezekiel, Liza, Jebediah.
Names without faces, faces without names.

Go back to Georgia, Kentucky, Tennessee, Maryland,
Virginia, up on over the border to Pennsylvania.
Go back over to the side you should have fought on.
Change the colour of your uniform,
change your vote, change the fate, un-buy those slaves,
uncrack the cowhide, unlick your lips, that hunger
you have for black skin to lash, your tongue a weapon,
quoting the Good Book, washing your hands clean in holy
                                                    water.

Leave the land to the Natives who know how to honour it.
Get back on that ship to England,
cross the channel back to France.
Take the Master out of Mister. Take off the H
you added to the family name. Return to your mother-
                                                    tongue,
parlez-vous again in the city you came from,
before they chased you out, or the grass got greener,
before the drought, the flood,
before some great great named John
went down with the ship called Increase,
before the long bitter of it all got passed down,
before the going down to the frozen ground
of the one without a name.

Call her Peace and let her rest. Amen.

Danielle Hope
A Trail of Stones

The first time she did not realise.
No guards. No check point.
No snipers posted in blank flats.
No queue shuffling forward.
No body search or sniffer dogs.
No passport required.

Later – like the leak suddenly spotted
by its stain in the ceiling, or the death
of a friend by a letter coming back –
she recognised she had crossed
to another country in the time taken
to push open a door.

So much the same, so much different.
Her tongue coiling in a strange
language, eyes misreading Made
for Mad. Always late, lost, the clasp
of her bag fallen open, her hair unravelled.
A genial people, giving generous food and wine
but also judging speech and silence
in prisons the tourists do not visit.

I do not belong. But three weeks later
she returns clutching fake papers.
East winds howl on the back of her neck.
Winter falls as she lays a trail of stones to find home.
And over months, like a llama crossing
mountains, time and again she picks a path
from one country to the other, grown sure-footed.
Now she says: *it is like changing clothes*
only what you shed is skin, a swift re-arrangement
of hair, the turn of our face.

Double agent, fighter for the resistance
she knows routes across the border
and the way from one self to the next.
But in her nightmares she wakes
and calls out in the wrong language
or loses the path of stones back
or fails to find the woman she left behind.

Peter Russell

Untitled

An empty bottle and a full ash-tray,
A feast of music in the memory,
Profoundest dialogue between us three –
A testimony to a well-spent day.
The others in the bar all went their way,
Nothing to say to our intensity –
They thought perhaps it was a merry spree
And not the language of the gods at play.

Moments like that are rare at any time –
You never know when magic intervenes
And all the squalid world transforms in bliss.
Dull brick itself sheds all its sordid grime,
And shining Parian appears with all its sheens –
Infinite light – on such a day as this.

Anne-Marie Fyfe

Storm Port

At times in the slow tepid night-hours
the walnut bed-frame slips anchor,
You steer by effort of will
in the lee of a Sacred Heart lamp
to the brocade-scalloped bay-
window, drown out the cantanker
of thinly-clad coathangers
in an oak wardrobe, the conspiring
of whispery neighbours at prayer.
At the bed's prow you discern the singing
of creeled lobsters as you lurch
evading unpaired shoes,
envelopes, an upended clothes-brush.
On the back-return landing, able
mariners stack beachtowels, sandbags,
fend jellyfish off in the stairwell, wait
for the Plimsoll mark to settle.

Frances Wilson

Widow

He used to say it was his favourite
Christmas present.   He dined out
for months on how he'd not get another
till he'd used it: the gravestone
I bribed two dustmen to rescue
from the dump and lug up our sideway
that winter they tidied the churchyard.

He planned to lay it, or to build
a feature, or a Folly but didn't
get round to it.   So it just stayed
leaning easily under the elder,
snail-trails and shadows crossing
its surface like memory;   sunbursts
of lichen showing our air was healthy,

its worn curlicues like arms
akimbo. It felt like a friend
waiting so we could peg out
our washing together.   Elizabeth.
I never knew if she was 'beloved'
or 'faithful' or even who she was
married to, and now even 'wife of'
is getting less and less certain.

Tony Turner

The Prague Lady

"Do you remember when freedom first came
Prague lady, Prague lady?"
"Oh yes, I remember when freedom first came",
Said the Prague lady.
"I was born into freedom back in `24
And I was so lucky to miss the Great War
Though my family were peasants, my family were poor,"
Said the Prague lady.

"Tell us what happened to freedom you had,
Prague lady, Prague lady."
"I'll tell you what happened to freedom we had,"
Said the Prague lady.
"That freedom was strangled by Browns and by Reds
With the bending of minds in impressionable heads
And my son and my husband were both gunned down dead,"
Sighed the Prague lady.

"And did you experience the liberation,
Prague lady, Prague lady?"
"Oh yes, I experienced the liberation,"
Said the Prague lady.
"It's when uniforms come that you think you can trust
but you end up enduring the rifleman's lust
flat on your back with your pride in the dust,"
Cried the Prague lady.

"And is it much better, once more to be free,
Prague lady, Prague lady?"
"Does it look so much better, is that what you see?"
Said the Prague lady.
"When the Communists came they said nothing's your own
So they gave me a job and they gave me a home
Now I can't find the rent and I'm old and alone,"
Wept the Prague lady

Carol Rumens

The Thingless Phrase

(To Edward Thomas, after reading 'The Word')

Though I'm not sure if I could recognise
The song from that of any rich-voiced bird,
Now you've marked for me something audible
As *pure thrush word,*
I wouldn't need to hear it twice,
I think, to trace the call
Out of that moment of parenthesis
(Not tuneful, *tart*; translatable to nothing
But un-romantic thrush-ness):
And if I never have the luck to hear
A thrush text-messaging,
It won't be lost, the mystery of your *thingless*
Name – I'll just keep coming back to where
The poem hears it, and wait there.

Sheenagh Pugh

Generosity

When I heard the slow disease
shake your notes, the tremolo
growing in your voice,

I thought back to how,
once, you sang a duet
on some TV chat show

with an old mate
whose voice was a ghost,
wrecked by tequila. Yet,

though its strength was lost,
the sweetness came over,
because you cut most

of the raw power
from your own, sang scarcely
above a murmur,

deferring tenderly
at every turn.
You'd think there might be

recompense; that even
illness and death might hanker
to match a gentleman
in such a gesture.

R.L. Cook

Lament

Now evening comes with cold and silent fingers,
　　Night billows down dark mist from greying sky;
Autumn is kindling where the last light lingers
　　And green-sick harvests quench the smouldering eye:
　　　　The house is ruined, weeds invade the floor,
　　　　For beauty does not walk here any more.

The trees are silent; all the birds have gone
　　And mildewed leaves deface the petalled way;
Through fading flesh the mocking, pointed bone,
　　Dusted with memory, marks the conscious clay
　　　　With winter blight, where summer flamed before,
　　　　For beauty does not walk here any more.

Never to watch the web of glory weave
　　Or feel the pulse of ripening in the veins;
Never again to breast the tides of love,
　　Only to wait, to drown in shrouding rains:
　　　　Ever to live, pocked by time's trammelling sore,
　　　　For beauty does not walk here any more.

Maggie Butt

Initiation

St Pancras Station, early Saturday,
clean and swept, airy as intention.

A fat man in a football shirt,
nylon, stripes of blue and white,
fit for a boat race, or a summer sky,
which stretches over cultivated belly
pregnant with beer and single mindedness.

If he were sliced as thin as pepperami
each slice would bear his team's name
flourishing, gothic script, like a stick of rock.

A small boy, skinny and baby-blonde,
swings on the railings, upside down,
dressed in the same sky strip; but in the genes
a slowly incubating photocopy of his dad.

The tiger's stripes are not just on his fur
but on the skin beneath.

Dad stops a passer-by and threateningly
menacing as a knife in a dark alley,
thrusts out a cheap disposable camera;
lines up beside his son, pats down his hair,
and grins with pride, a pork-pie smile.

A dream fulfilled – me and my boy –
his first match, great initiation
into the soaring hope and dark despair
it means to be a man.

Susan Wicks

Blue

This sea is so blue it is
all seas. The separate waves home in,
a layered ache of colour.
Every tide ever turning
has marked this one breakwater.
A gull's cry pierces and pierces
as the sand trickles
into itself, a long shimmer
to the rising floor. A crabshell
gives up its several dead.

Where is she? my father asks me
of my mother, five years cremated
and scattered. Why doesn't she write?

Blue on blue, with every tide
the colour deepens. Only, far out,
a blink, a sudden dazzle –
that gap in the horizon
where sun melts it to nothing,
remakes it white and empty.

Leonie Rushforth

Winter Colours

at first it looks like an old photograph
pale and faded under a different sun,
boundaries between things
uncertain

after a while, it becomes clear
these are the city's winter colours
and the city is seasonal
still

though even the cars and small lorries
are white and shades of grey

there are no hoardings anywhere
some signs are yellow,
some red, but these are not
overbearing

I begin to rest my eyes in the paleness
in which people move dressed
in darker tones

Peter Russell

Divine Love

In sweeter mood and temper now
Than I have known for years,
I think of past loves' torments, how
They ground me down to tears.
In this Old People's Home I've found
My heart by sheer Compassion crowned.

Roy Davids

White Noise

Shostakovitch had a special friend
whom he could telephone to come
and spend some time with him.
No words would pass between them;
they would just sit silently across the room:
Shostakovitch solid as in his photograph.
After half an hour, he would thank
the friend, who would then get up and leave.
What he needed was the company,
not conversation; just not to be alone;
to have the sense of someone being there.
Perhaps it was telepathy? A transference
back and forth? A therapy? Sounds
outside our human reach and range?

Most of what elephants communicate
we feel but cannot hear; it is too deep
for us, though they can pick it up five miles away.
We do not hear white noise but know it's there,
covering over silence – like dust in air,
only seen in sunlight. It protects us,
and our inner lives;
in part allows our sense of self.

Often less than music half unheard,
because not really listened to;
lighter than laughter through a wall
or children in the gardens down the hill;
it is like a picture not noticed till removed;
can be as slight as half the senses; a feeling –
almost beyond the rim of consciousness.
We seek out that comfort as our norm –

need a pulse of sympathy out there.
Silence can leave us anxious
empty
too aware.

Might much of what is meant by love
be best described as noise that's white?

Peter Dale

Making Peace

The desert's unforgiving.
    The last time they came
        They bulldozed its dust
Over the living.
    They set the torrid air aflame
        And said the war was just.

The long arm of their law.
    They thought they were
        The world's police.
Quick on the draw,
    They never heard
        Ozymandias keep the peace.

Michael Newman

Stations of a Lesser Cross

When the last flame
Flickers
In the improbable bonfire,
And the full moon
Lifts off
Over the thatched roof;

When Dives and Lazarus
Plays
On Classic FM,
And the children
Hush
To a bedtime fable;

When orange blossom
Scents out
The midnight garden,
And stars pinpoint
Our provisional knowledge:

Have we come at last
To an unlikely Paradise,
The serenity of seeing
Beyond false expectation? –
To what is,
And only can be?

David Perman
Double Take

Yes it was frightening but exciting too.
We ran across fifty metres of open ground
– *oh at least a hundred* – right in front
of their guns. It was a miracle they didn't
open fire. My hair stood on end.
I had goose pimples all over.

The papers we carried cost us a week's
rations – a year's wages *– and the clothes*
were too big, too baggy. Certainly too big..
They smelled foreign but everything that
went on was foreign.

We hid in straw, under piles of vegetables.
At the border soldiers poked with their sticks –
not sticks, they were bayonets – poking deep, this way and that.
One of them tore my sleeve. Here's the tear, the scratch.

Then we were shut up for eighteen hours –
more like 24 – in that metal container
without bread or water. *Precious little air.*
Forbidden to talk or move in case
they heard us. *It was creepy –*
in case the guards heard us.

When we reached these shores, people couldn't
believe we had done it. I went to the Palace and was decorated.
When we reached these shores, I was detained,
sent to a camp in the north country.

I was a hero, I had escaped from an evil enemy.
Now I am a magistrate. I uphold the rule of law.

I was an asylum seeker escaping persecution
I had faith in this country's rule of law.

You are <u>at best</u> an economic migrant, at worst
unhealthy, immoral, perhaps criminal
even a terrorist
we must send you back.

I am an asylum seeker, fleeing an evil enemy.

No.   <u>We</u> were the ones who fled the evil enemy.
<u>You</u> are a sponger.

<u>You</u> are an oppressor.

We have nothing in common.
We will send you back.

Keith McFarlane

From the Window

A mist fell from the autumn sky
and lent the bare limbs modesty;
where all before was sharp and cold
the leaves of burgundy and of gold
were cloaked in soft perplexity:
so seemed the scene change to my eyes.

Each lamp that once was harsh and bright
and fired with fierce modernity
became with haloes ringed, suffused
with softness: gas mantled flames burned thus
by night a hundred years ago
when stones first rose above this site.

The moon came up, drew back the pall
and touched the trees, each twig and branch,
with silver etched on velvet sky:
the beauty of the living root, why
even in the city's neon heart
a moment can become eternal.

Peter Porter

Instructions for Dream Dialling

You have reached the Voice Mail of the Soul –
if you wish to be connected to the dream
press the button marked 'Anxiety';
if you require the services of 'The Moral
Monitor', or desire to be told 'A Fable
of the Future', touch the 'Integration tab';
if 'Apocalypse', 'Arcadia', or 'Anomy'
are in your remit, return to the switchboard
and seek further assistance; if, instead,
you subscribe to 'Erotopia' or 'Psychothesia'
key in the number on your Member's Card;
if you are entitled to a rebate on the 'Ordinary',
the 'Commonplace' or have been designated 'Everyday',
ignore all other instructions and follow guidelines
in the official 'Theophrastian Handbook';
otherwise ask to be put through either
to 'Contingency' or 'Insomnia'.

June Hall

Three Solos

A Mother's Response to Mr Eliot

One: Morning

I

Plans past and plans future
both perhaps sour plans present.
What might have been and what has been
lead to one conclusion –
a mother's place is in the wrong.

II

Round the still point of the manic morning
whirls the early Monday chaos –
homework, sick notes, hockey sticks,
racquets, morning snacks, back packs –
swirled from hall to fridge to bedroom,
the hunt for cartons of juice and lost trainers.
Distracted from reaction by reaction,
inoperancy of co-operation,
desecration of the inner sanctum,
the wail of disconsolate children.

III

That was a way of putting it – not very child-friendly.
At this point there is only the clock
– which says eight. Go, go, go say the kids.
Their voices in the back
scrabble, squeal, disagree. We're late
moving yet hardly moving in half-filled jeeps
that block the slow flow over the bridge.
See the faces brushed by terror,
see the road rage simmering –

not here, not the silence of deep sleep,
not the dead hush of the empty house.

IV
I drop them on a double yellow
breathing relief into cold air.
To arrive is to undo all our worrying
and know we've made it for another day.

V
The pram is in the hall.
The fog is in the fir tree.
A gym-slip sleeps on the briar rose.

Sibling jeers and slaps echo in the mind
down the hours of sleep never taken,
the plans never realised.

Two: Afternoon

I
In my morning is my afternoon,
in my afternoon my morning.
What might have been – meditation,
sun-tanning, novels, working late –
and what has been
remain a perpetual possibility in a child-free world.

II
So here I am in the middle of my life,
entre les années de liberté,
having largely wasted the magic of motherhood
measuring out my life with school runs.
Missed dates and unfulfilled goals
point to one cause
which is always overload.

III
In my pink-paint-peeling kitchen
I had not thought so much undone.
Ketchup-smeared plates, discarded crusts,
half-drunk bottles, blobs of jam,
crumbs and whirled bits of paper
smear and trash the space.
Plans before and plans after.

Clucking from one appointment to the next
mother love cannot bear too much triviality.

IV
A time for the afternoon pick-up,
A time for tea and a time for television.
Quick, now, here, now, Mummy, say the kids
demanding complete absorption.
Quick! Quick! Quick!
Hungry children cannot wait,
not now with the wink of the microwave
and the flat face of the wide screen blinking.

A time for homework and a time for play.
The clash of voices and slamming doors
all lead to one end
which is usually crossness.
Muddy feet tramping,
up and down, in and out,
mirth of youth, before the crease of wrinkles
and the slow slide into stodge.

Three: Evening

1
After the tear-swept bedtime
when the bath-water's chilled and

the last battles waged and truces struck
will small fingers encircle my neck,
clutch and cling?

Will these children
drift into angel sleep?
Makura Om. Peace upon the pillow.

II
I shall not cease from exploration –
byeways and back roads, rat runs and cut-throughs –
and the end of all my commuting
will be to arrive where I started –
home – and see it for the first time.

III
Here, now, in the failing light
destiny is homebound and child-centred,
destiny is drawn in peanut butter.
When tiredness and headaches are one
and the roar of lost tempers fades
I slump upon the bed,
a condition of complete depletion
not uncommon in parents.

IV
But all will be fine
and all sorts of things will be fine
when clouds pass and reflections in the pool deepen,
young faces smile like sunflowers turned to me
or wild roses opening under the apple tree,
when the house is filled with laughter,
the sound of mine infolded with theirs
and the joy and the journey are one.

John Cotton

The Lives of Poets

I am going to give up
Reading the lives of poets,
They are too depressing!
Why do they turn out to be
Crypto Fascists, anti-Semites,
Fantasists believing in fairies or astrology,
Season ticket holders for funny farms,
Curmudgeonly onanists,
Boozers and bed-wetters,
Or serial shaggers
Of other men's wives?
Why can't they live reasonable
And less tragic lives?
But then I suppose they'd write
Worthy and forgettable poems.

Katherine Gallagher

At Delphi

Clouded Yellows, Red Admirals, others I cannot name
weaving in and out of bindweed, daisies, buttercups.
They've flown over wide sea-stretches
to reach these wild grasses, tombs and ruins.

I breathe the scented air, feel the sky's silk,
there for the taking. I can almost unknot
my unhappiness – see how its underside
is the impossible love
I've carried all this way
like spare, necessary baggage.

Can I ungrip it, leave it here
for random gods to give one last blessing?
I hear your voice urging me on
to walk through this
steady fire of butterflies.

Mercer Simpson

The Somnambulist

I am a man who, in a dream,
walks in his sleep to touch the face of time.
He cannot reach the frontier of his theme:
he cannot give his waking place a name.

But that knifed waking is thrombosis on the stairs,
the blood-stained cupboard and the roaring gas:
Though I, the sleeper, am who never was,
am free as silence underneath the stars.

Michael Croshaw

Sad Hour

This time of night you would find them at the club,
paying outrageous prices
and having their ears dinned.
They are there to meet others like themselves
adrift and wanting comfort:
which means conversation
then dancing drunkenly till they fall down.
A taxi that costs the moon and stars
brings them the few miles home,
where they groan back to life next day in Sabbath hell.

If you could stand the crowd, the noise, the stink,
you would see these hothouse plants come to brief
                                          bright bloom
before they and another foul week go.
There's frenzy there, born of failure and frustration,
as from the dance floor rise the fragments of dreams
that try to be whole again, in someone's arms,
while the world's a whirlpool, a mixing
of darkness and flashing lights,
and tears flow fast and helpless
in the joy of misery, for one sad hour.

Nicholas Bartholomew

Soap Operas And The Community

Indoors, we watch
these characters on
the television, these
strangers we call friends
on streets we know
with enough familiarity
to be able to call home...

    ... while outside, we walk
    through streets we
    barely recognise.

Indoors, we sit around
the television and cheer
the good guys, boo and hiss
the bad guys, laugh at their
quirks, pity them their
weaknesses, envy them
their strengths...

    ... while outside, we stride,
    head down, eyes averted,
    shunning unwanted attention.

Indoors, we discuss
the lives and worries and
troubles of characters
who are mere vapours,
illusions on the telly,
created by writers,
portrayed by actors...

    ... while outside the community
    fades and withers away like
    an un-watered plant.

Joanna Preston

Limbo

This is the space he has inhabited, since
"there's nothing we can do. I'm sorry."

He said he felt it flare out from his body
slamming doctor and desk and hospital bed,
the walls of the consultant's room

back and away, leaving him teetering
the centre of an expanding void.

     *   *   *

No whole-family picnics next summer, no point
saving money for a cruise to the Islands.

What will we do with the trees for the orchard?
– he won't plant them. He says their slender trunks
remind him of the long-legged schoolgirl I was.

At night, he holds me so tightly
I have bruises by the morning.

     *   *   *

He says it's like being in a crazed glass bubble.
Distorted. No warmth can reach him.

He's sitting on the verandah, the cat sprawled
across his legs, belly curved towards the sun
"... I've tried to be a good man ..."
He doesn't seem aware of weeping,

and all I can think of
is insects, trapped in amber.

Mario Petrucci

Fence

(Chernobyl, 1986)

This side of the fence
is clean. That side
dirty. Understand?

You must forget
that soil is like skin.
Or interlocking scales

on a dragon. Dirty.
Clean – is all that matters
here. Imagine a sheet

of glass coming down
from the sky. It's easy
no? On this side

you can breathe
freely. Your cow can
eat the grass. You can

have children. That side
you must wear a mask
and change the filter

every four hours.
You ask – What if my cow
leans over the fence?

Personally I say
it depends which end. But
we have no instructions

for that. It is up to you
to make sure your cow
is not so stupid.

The Breath

Not impossible is it? Or even
unlikely. That a bus conductor

    leaned from his step that day, craned
east round the corner of his pole

    and took it. Or that a young woman
punching air with the news

    of her promotion struck out
for an early lunch – much earlier

    than she might have done – and
throwing her head back in triumph

    took it. Or that a boy held his lolly
up to the sun for comparison and

    at its resonant lemon – gasped.
And took it. Or that some incoming

    dispatch crackled my radio which I
lifted to the sill (raising the sash

    for better reception) which is why
I was standing by that open window

    so under-informed – so maybe it was
me who took it, liable as any

    conductor, woman, boy who didn't
take it at all, just me – half-cut with

    the dusk for Christ's sake – bet it
was, knowing my bum luck, knowing

    me – when it might have sunk sizzling
into the gutter or made some privet leaf

grow backwards or something – but
the odds are still on my side – aren't

they? – with me, whose breath maybe
didn't slide in that day with its fizzing

speck of cargo, to bank in my lung
its bastard atom. So not me after

all? Not impossible. Is it. Or even
unlikely? That I didn't? Didn't take

that one wrong breath.

Roy Davids

Silent Movie

The sky is flawless cobalt,
though leaves, burnt orange,
shake wildly in the bitter wind.
Everything is crisp –
new snow, twigs underfoot,
all conversation.
The day insists on itself
and those who venture out
melt into something marvellous
– like birds' silhouettes
dipping silently in the lake.

Ruth O'Callaghan

Love Sections

When the magi come for her she does not move
the baby, slung loosely over her shoulder,
unwilling to release him
to the confines of the pen.
Her blanched fingers swab the door-frame,
dribbling bleach, the drum stands whitely, sofa high:
Not to be taken internally:
Keep well away from children.

When the dark doctor, smelling of olibanum
and wild camomile, coughs
the mother sashays backwards, shoots
a killing stream of germicide
from her child-bearing hip.

Placating, the social worker finger-tickles
the baby's splayed foot,
his cold wedding ring
curves the pliant body.
Lovingly, the mother scours the spot.

The psychiatrist helps stash the once-worn baby
clothes into sacks, as big and black as body bags,
his balsam words ease the baby
from her arms, persuade her the germs are snared.
Together they tourniquet the top,
straitening the mother's love:
Not to be taken internally
Keep well away from children.

Rhona McAdam
Sunday Driving

Then your father took the wheel
honking and thrusting into traffic
nosing the arse of the car in front
plunging out of lane to pass
and flashing his high beams
at the cars too slow to MOVE!

And my mother yelled at him
with all the words she swallowed,
all the holiday road trips
she suffered, all the driving
that scared her.   But now she's dead
it's easier to speak her mind.

Your father, also dead, declines
to answer, punching his way
round your skull;   fixing road, cars,
woman drivers with his bead:
he hates them all would they get
out-of-his-WAY? My mother,
silenced, watches the sunset
and headlights in the mirror.

Little left to say to one another
these two, their parents'
words stopped in their throats.

Martyn Crucefix
Dolmen at Skyber Hen

One of the last molars of the county
peers through misted windows to where
we spend a candlelit Christmas Day

in a converted barn we treat as home,
eating Turkish Delight, liqueur trifles,
kiwi and kumquat and dates,

the cream and purple of ham on the bone,
high octane chocolate, nuts
and berries so far beyond the staple.

Its shadowy, toothy crenellations
bring back days of hunt and kill, pulling
down blood in this brief daylight,

yet we celebrate the new religion –
grown old in just two thousand years,
so my own children hesitate to name

the mother and father of Jesus Christ.
They cannot say why a weakling child
was born in straw like a sacrifice.

The giving of gifts is a simpler delight.
And the excess of everything makes
more sense under the dolmen's weight,

unmoved beneath stars we see tonight
without the blind of civilisation.
So one comes in breathless with cold,

with starlight in her lungs as if to say
prodigality gives rise to its own
gestures: a reply to ice-plates, stiffened

slush and mud's miracle of iron crust,
the wind's sheaf of sharpened knives –
every bitter provocation to give more

and more than we can reasonably afford –
useless in the end, though it will resound
long after these older, equivocal gifts.

Brian Patten

Grim Comfort

Not knowing what they did, the dead
Taught me how best I should live
Out the days denied to them:

As simply as the marigold
As simply as the weightless wren.

They also taught me how,
When I am become part of them

I will not miss the marigold
Or the weightless, singing wren

Julia Deakin

Twentieth Century

This is my aunt, my great aunt Nellie Brown
(who lived, for what it was worth, to 101)
before her given name became a joke
standing at fifteen in the sea at Rhyl
some 20 feet from her younger sister's
photographic paraphernalia.

Her mother beside her looks unsure
but Nellie stands at ease – with life, with the breeze,
with the unfamiliar feel of her calves exposed to the sun
and the tickling surf: she looks us in the eye,
flexes her toes in the sand and sees who knows what
beyond the camera before her.

My aunt, before the twentieth century was born
when Rhyl was a day's jaunt in the charabanc
before the omnibus or motor car; before she saw
her grandmother burn in her nightdress by the hearth;
before they built the red brick market hall
at which the whole town kissed its youth goodbye.

My aunt, before she joined the VAD
before Edouard's last postcard from the front
before her brother came back maimed and silent;
before her sister's tumour let her claim
her niece and nephew and – in vain – their father;
before she nursed her parents to their slow deaths.

Before she took in the evacuees who would not eat,
before her brother turned to drink
and fathered a child she would not speak of,
before she kept house forty years for him
before she took in two stray cats for company
before the waiting rooms, the waiting lists...

before the home help helped herself
before the Queen misspelled her name
before the day and nightly moaning
from the next bed in the nursing home...
Before all this, before the breaking waves
my aunt stands, clutching her sepia petticoats
                                        knee high,
seeing a life that ripples and sparkles before her
and she smiles.

John Mole

The Way It Was

No choice. You went into the firm because the firm
Was waiting for you. That's the way it was.
Why allowed no answer other than because.
Because I say so. It's your turn.
And so my father did as he was told,
Making the best of it against the grain.
He buckled down. He wouldn't ask again.
The dreams I know he had were put on hold.

They held for life and never let him go.
The doctor he had hoped to train to be
Made of his practice of accountancy
A curative release. To him I owe
All I'm still learning from a selfless man
Who let me go my way, be what I am.

Mark Leech

A Short Poem About Love

When the evening is just ordinary,
no troubles worse than work and sleepiness
no wonders more than tea and sitting down
you surprise me with a smile.
                              The world grows
beyond itself and I fall out of things
into first love again, as though my shells
of habit and thinking have disappeared.

A single star, sign of a universe
supporting this, brimming with tenderness.

Jacqui Shapiro

No-Man's-Land

and so,
my little one,
it is beginning.

In that case,
let us prepare.

I give you
the easy thrill
of mascara, the
instant lipstick smile,
the familiar terrain of

your hair swept into new
arrangements, the silk of your mother's
skirt, loose and proud against your skin.

Stilettoed, balancing,
you walk, swaying at the hips.
In perfumed fog, thick with promise,
you turn, you pose, you grow breasts.

I have been to that
no-man's-land you now
inhabit, that holding place
between one age and the next.
I too have known impatience, but
understand this. I have walked the
treacherous road ahead which you
must travel alone. And there are dangers;

beyond this still circle lies
the land of infinite longings,
a kingdom of fear and desire
where novice hearts beat and bleed,
beat and bleed, amid great movements of earth,
storms and high winds and darkness, amid rare and
precious days of light and silence and perfect moments of
                                        grace.

I was there.
You'll find my footprints.
Salt and earth, bile and blood,
milk and bone, stay with me a while.
Sooner or later, you will be gone.
And so my little one,
let us prepare.

Alison Chisholm
Leda's Learning

'So mastered by the brute blood of the air ,
Did she put on his knowledge with his power .....?'
from 'Leda and the Swan' by William Butler Yeats

Can you imagine how I felt that day?
I hardly understood what happened, how
that huge white bird could take me. For a while
I prayed it was a nightmare: but I knew
those strange marks where his bill secured my neck,
the feathers in my hair, the pain ... the pain ...
were real. And now I feel a fluttering,
a quickening of child or bird within,
and future fears outweigh the horrors past.
For how can I confide in anyone?
What women's lore will show me what to do?
Who will I turn to when the time arrives?

It seems my torture made me more aware:
my senses all seem heightened. I can hear
a swan's egg crack in nests a mile away,
can feel the earth worms wriggling in soil,
see still pools stirred by breezes, and can smell
lush water weed, and crave to swallow it.

More strange, each hour that passes fills my head
with knowledge people strive for, and the gods
alone should have. Today I understand
the infinite variety of birds,
and start to feel how mountain, copse and sea
emerged from swirling chaos of the earth.
Tomorrow I will know how stars and moon
hang in the night sky; how it all began.

A new fear overtakes me. When I shed
my burden, will I keep this learning? Or
will I become an empty husk, dead shell,
impoverished detritus of the gods?

Roy Davids

Fish

They are the jewels
of the necklace of water.

They are the pearls
of the deeper pools

They are the diamonds
in the waterfall's hair.

Duncan Forbes

Sloe Gin

The taste reminds me
of being young again.
The stained-glass thimbleful
of purple liquid
is sweet and pungent on the tongue
and the taste is not of plums
but wild blackthorn fruit
picked mature from hedgerows
after the first frosts of autumn.

I am in my grandmother's house.
I have in my hand a glass
of her home-made sloe gin
and we are listening
to Paul Robeson sing
on a wind-up gramophone
as big as a pulpit
while I at eight or nine
am certain what it will be
to feel grown up.

Sloe gin and Old Man River.
The bushes have flowered
and petals fallen
for half a century since then.

Simon Zonenblick

Bargain Hunt

I needed a gun to kill some kids
And murder some refugees,
It was taking too long for them to die
Of starvation and disease.

"I know a woman," I was told,
"Though you'll be lucky if you catch her.
She's a bit of a jet-setting, footloose old bird
Her name is Maggie Thatcher.

She sells 'em by the thousands,
Her deals are really good.
Bombs, grenades, whatever you need
To spill some innocent baby's blood!"

I went to the place where he said she'd be,
And, do you know, she wasn't there!
Still, I found someone else who was just as good.
His name was Tony Blair.

Andrew Motion

Due North

Outside the dainty igloo
Surrounded by desert snow
Footprints come and go.

But neither hide nor hair
Of any inhabitants there
Impress the swirling air.

Is it one person or two?
If anyone ever knew
They noticed, then withdrew.

Now there is only me,
And I can no longer see
Truth with certainty.

I am too cold to feel,
So much an imbecile
Real becomes unreal.

I open my mouth to speak
And a misty fizzle breaks
Away in a silent shriek.

I hold my breath and hear
The chorus of the spheres
Shrivelling in my ears.

But outside the dainty igloo
Surrounded by desert snow
Footprints come and go.

They do. I told you so.

William Oxley

Just One

Come, let us lie down together
a short time in the mud
and love will make it forever.
Never mind the rats and blood
and everyday diseases of reason,
in truth life has but a short season.
Lie down, love, in the body's
fading beauty, your hair
to me, lips and hands, all
will be perpetually fair;
not one thing will ever pall
despite this cold, damp life of envy
and unjustness. Though dark
is always near and heavy,
yet there are stars starring the black;
and though mouths choke with tears
at all the polluted ways of days,
long since we blended our two fires
to make one blaze that stays
even the cold shiver of death's
breathlessness. So come, let us lie down,
now, and for always, just one.

U.A. Fanthorpe

FWIW: The Language Speaks

HWAET!
Was brought to the island
Over bitter waters
By rowers wielding longswords.
Adam-like named a new world –
Oak, grass, hand, foot, house, sheep, sea.
(Rivers, having their old names,
Churlishly refused my choices.)

HARO!
Smote them at Senlac
The Prince and the people.
Taught them our fashions –
Judge, justice, penalty,
Prison and Parliament,
Fine arts of peacetime,
Gentleman, beauty. April.

HEY NONNY!
Found words everywhere. They came at my calling,
Names for the know-it-alls, arbiter, genius;
And for know-nothings, ignoramus, inertia;
Measurers wanted pendulums, axis and nucleus;
Thinkers craved curriculum and its callow offspring;
Doctors found bacillus, lens, equilibrium;
Travellers asked for omnibus. Got terminus as well.

HEY GUYS!
Shall we move the goalposts?
Try a level playing-field? No wow there.
Use a buzz-word, bog-standard wannabe
Sex it up? Stay shtumm? Oh, the great

Orchestra of English, played in every key,

Gobsmacked! *Good* hair day! Where we're at!
In a right Horlicks! Braggadocious!

    f w i w (for what it's worth).

R.V. Bailey

Recycling Facility

What shall I do with this? the old lady asks,
Offering a telephone. *It still works.*
Not now, it doesn't! He chucks it in a skip.

Such casual ruthlessness disturbs: the ovens,
The quick-lime pits... But we drive away
Lightened, delivered – a new start, a clean slate?
Something about poverty, chastity, even obedience calls.

Simplicity's not for us. Merely living
Brings in its wake a tide of rubbish we can't wait
To bin. Recycling's the word that makes it OK
To throw so many things away.
Is nothing meant to last?

What should we do with these, the old,
The bad, the helpless?
They still work.

Mimi Khalvati

Ghazal

If I am the grass and you the breeze, blow through me.
If I am the rose and you the bird, then woo me.

If you are the rhyme and I the refrain, don't hang
on my lips, come and I'll come too when you cue me.

If yours is the iron fist in the velvet glove
when the arrow flies, the heart is pierced, tattoo me.

If mine is the venomous tongue, the serpent's tail,
charmer, use your charm, weave a spell and subdue me.

What shape should I take to marry your own, have you –
hawk to my shadow, moth to my flame – pursue me?

If I rise in the east as you die in the west,
die for my sake, my love, every night renew me.

If, when it ends, we are just good friends, be my Friend,
muse, brother and guide, Shamsuddin to my Rumi.

Be heaven and earth to me and I'll be twice the me
I am, if only half the world you are to me.

Ann Drysdale

The Case for Light Verse

For John Whitworth

Beside the epic, with its long tradition
Of mythic reference and erudition,
Darling of bards po-faced and reverential,
Light verse seems horribly inconsequential.
There is no literary substance to it,
No lasting value; any fool can do it.
Take up the burden that distorts your soul,
Crack it and tip it out into a bowl;
Discard the yolk and then with merry vigour
Whip up the white and add a bit of sugar.
This is a recipe that can't go wrong;
A little biscuit melting on the tongue,
Tickling the idiot's fancy like a feather
Making him laugh and clamour for another.
No one expects us amiable asses
To seek to reach the peak of Mount Parnassus,
Therefore, dear heart, let us write fast and louche
And give the common man his *amuse-bouche.*
Write light. Let rip with a poetic fart.
That way they may conclude we have no heart
But those who really matter will know better..

John Whitworth

No Can Do

You can empty the Nile with a shovel,
You can climb to the moon up a rope,
You can bat in the nude at the Oval,
You can model Atlantis in soap,
You can share a cigar with the devil,
Then enjoy a blind date with the pope
Where you sip aftershave from your navel
Sky-high on that Vatican dope,

> *But you can't get your kids out the bathroom,*
> *Though you grouse and you gripe and you mope.*
> *If your kids are booked into the bathroom*
> *You had better abandon all hope.*

You can train your twin ferrets to answer the phone,
You can see that they do it in Greek,
You can drum on your bum with a dinosaur bone,
If you think it improves your physique,
You can seethe like a haggis in eau-de-Cologne
Then hang from a hook for a week,
You can moan all alone in a coffin of stone
(It's an old meditation technique),

> *But you can't get your kids out the bathroom,*
> *Though you wail and you whinge and you shriek.*
> *When your kids relocate to the bathroom*
> *Then your personal hygiene looks bleak.*

You can drink 'em as fast as they pour 'em
And stand every time that you fall,
You can lose every sense of decorum
And behave like a bear in a brawl,

You can sing to the stars cockalorum
From a perch on the nunnery wall,
Then finish the night with a jorum
And drop off to sleep in the hall,

> *But you can't get your kids out the bathroom,*
> *Though you yowl and you yell and you bawl,*
> *Still your chances of using the bathroom*
> *Are infinitesimally small.*

> *No you can't get your kids out the bathroom,*
> *There will always be kids in the bathroom,*
> *When your kids are staked out in the bathroom,*
> *THEN YOU CAN'T USE THE BATHROOM AT ALL!*

Wendy French

The Concert Pianist

for years
he played faithfully this b minor
          he now taps on the windowsill
memories that grew with him

ebony finished steinways
iron wrought balconies champagne in intervals

bow ties
his mother's smile
        looking up from her piano
and her photograph
always and still
        next to his bed

too young to understand
when she'd left he'd been content
with letters
        envelopes

coloured stamps koala bears

but now this chord
always this chord (she'd played over and over again)
haunts his waking dreams
his sleeping hours

and tomorrow
two male nurses
        will accompany him
as the minister takes him to the chapel and as it is easter

he will be
   triumphant allowed to play

passing through a mist of empty flower beds
this open walk will lead him

                         to a god who listens to voices imitate
the sane and he will deliver a chopin prelude to a captive
                                       congregation
who choose shuffling from locked wards to this resurrection
and days echoing that first cold morning

Peggy Poole

Visiting Jill

All goes onward and outward, nothing collapses
And to die is different from what anyone supposes...
— Walt Whitman

In evening sunlight I come to be beside your grave
where waving grasses emphasise the green
diminish the starkness of raw earth.

It is six weeks since your wicker coffin
threaded with wild flowers
was lowered here.   Funeral wreaths are wilted.

Birds sing and the breeze
broadcasts a dove's liquid call
a winged requiem.

Dandelion, bluebell and celandine,
willow and hawthorn keep you company.
Dock leaves flourish at my feet.
A thistle spreads its early growth.
Sitting on an old beech stump
I notice the shrub someone has planted.

Squirrels are chasing
across the grass.   They do not
look at all afraid.

Today your grave is overgrown with grasses,
their tips feather the evening air.
Thistle is shoulder high and menacing.
Shrub has been overwhelmed.   I cannot
.   find it. Wind hisses through full-leafed trees,
makes shadows skim the ground.

Lodged against a thorn
the white froth of cuckoo spit.
Larvae protection.

Sycamore seeds surprise; I touch some of pallid green,
rosy pink on another branch. I've only ever seen them
brown, miniature planes of autumn landings.

On the stump Painted Lady waits and Speckled Wood
clings to long grass. As I leave Small White circles
my head. I remember how you brought butterflies to art.

Distant traffic thrum
is background to the stillness.
Life driving ahead.

Early autumn leaves begin to drop; your glade's
been manicured; earth is scarred by tractor tracks.
Two new companions have come:

Sheila and 'darling Caroline' whose 'Ma and Da'
left a sheath of nineteen kinds of shrubs and trees.
Late lunchtime. Bird song. High sun.

All the nettles droop.
Have they at last lost their sting?
I choose not to test.

In December dusk I return; find new grass,
a yellow primula, dead leaves on sodden ground,
as tracery of branches patterns grey sky.

After earth's other busy seasons
this green space breathes affirmation.
Nothing here speaks of an end...

Peter Porter

An End to Envy

The end will come only with the end
of everything, but we must work at it.
We start by imagining a level space
into which the personality
is pressed, a pouting flower contiguous
with solitude, a practised train of leaves
endlessly advantaged by the sun.
We are given evolutionary skill
at being just ourselves, God's new Ark,
his smallest snail, his globe of nothings.
Then, as if the skin of life were hardening,
we become the domicile of species
and a pompous programme wills we send
our sensual love to settle in a world of beauty,
a world our eyes have sworn to see
through every aperture.
                                    Everything
is being changed and everything
is irreplaceable: we are assessments
of what has hardened out of vapour, has played
the series of the good and bad prosthesis
and wondered why the artificial is
more truthful than the natural. We are
an average of what the mighty and
the minuscule endure. There'll come a verb
which joins the gifted to the glib:
by this deceit we'll want for no-one's
charm or beauty; we'll be seen as torches
of ourselves, conscious merely
that our envy is the solstice of our praise.

Rose Flint

October Blessing

The leaves are blessing me, the falling leaves
are blessing me and the road, the falling fiery leaves
are generous with their blessings and include
my old silver Saab, a Dalmatian, the tax inspector
hurriedly crossing his camomile lawn and a slow-worm
coiled like a copper torc in her sun-bliss by the rockery.

I have only to stand still and October blesses me
with her dry lizardy kisses; my arms are touched,
my white lifted face is touched briefly, delicately
bless, bless, bless ... months caress me with their fortunes,
a whole year of months. I reach out joyously to all
this goldleaf rain, these papery dollars of light, this luck.

This winter will bring blessing even under ice, under snow
and sorrow. In my own boulevard the tax inspector and I
will be blessed with lucks printing their sudden colours
on our roads and careful lawns, the hound's coming and

going.
The sleeping slow worm will teach me how to hoard
the leaves warmth and let their light filter into my heart,
leaching out the old year's toxins so we will wake in the green
Spring, shrug off the dust of our last skin and begin again.

Lynne Wycherley

Child of Stromness

i.m. of George Mackay Brown

i
The bell tips its small horizon,
a metal shiver of freedom.
Slates are discarded,
chalks roll their dust.
Beyond the school gate
a green wind hurries the grass,
the tide's bright glaze.

Sleeves flapping, you skitter
down the street.   No doors
between you and island-light,
long shores, June's
wide-eyed blue: you could fly.

Above Stromness, the brae –
a humpback whale arching with joy.

ii
A racked adolescence:
breath in instalments,
the rasp, the hack, the pain.
Now you are a thin flame
in a long white ward.

Wrecks redden in Scapa Flow,
thirst with rust.   You make
your berth between sheet and ale.

Daffodil women sail the street
with April in their arms.
They float through your beer jar,

lissom as porpoises,
unattainable as stars.

iii
Muirburn: heather on fire.
You reach for Woodbines, Burns.
Words fall through your parched sky,
fulmars, pintails, terns.

iv
Sleet-grey walls, metal stairs.
A fan-heater by your kitchen table.
A cigarette wags its shadow,
writes in small cairns.
Poem by poem, the islands
sing their circles on your page.

v
You hang your star in a pane,
the one small window on the sea.
What does it frame?
A few salt inches.
Red gravel clearing its throat.
Rowing boats: halved fruit
peeling yellow, serge, white.

vi
Outside your death I find you,
a splinter of light
still lodged among stones,
the swerving grey mile of Stromness.

Storm-coloured groove,
your life ran its course

flagstone by flagstone
from museum to ale-house,
lifeboat to kirkyard, its sides
whetted by Atlantic winters,
the emery of your passing.

vii
I walk past alleyways,
the ghosts of sweet shops,
sherbet and claggam,
Ferry Road, Creig's Pier
where a boy that is you
dangles a line, dances
a sillock's tin flash.

Fred Beake
Elegy

Disdain not the valour of young men who go
    to war, knowing the consequence
and return with sordid nightmares in their souls
    having done hard things, that evil
might not flourish, and dark shadows fall.
    And if some revelled in the adventure
and wandered out of their way by the gorges of death
    that was always the right of the young.
And if this death or that was harsh or pointless
    do not talk too easily of waste.

Ruth Fainlight
Crocuses

These crocuses are appalling:
pale, bare, tender stems rising
through the muddy winter-faded turf,

shivering petals the almost luminous mauve
of lurid bruises on the frightened faces
and naked bodies of men, women, children

herded into a forest clearing or
towards a siding where a train has halted
    and the trucks are waiting.

an earlier version of the poem which later appeared in Burning Wire. *See acknowledgements*

Alan Murray

Lately

Yes, it all seems real enough:
this café where we meet from time to time,
still friends, just as we'd promised;
the tree across the road outside the church,
its bare branches silhouetted on the wall
forming webs of shadow and substance;
that uninvited moon,
loitering with obscure intent
in the awkward silence of a clear mid-morning sky.
Yes, I can't deny it looks the part.

At our table by the door,
I listen to you talk of people I don't know
and plans I'm not a part of,
noting how, in all your tales and stories,
I have slipped from 'is' to 'was',
or some uncertain, not-quite-present tense,
unknown to grammar or ontology.
And as I search for some last trace of me
in what you say,
I watch my faint reflection in the window
and cannot shake this sense that I've outlived myself,
that I've become this disincarnate something
lingering here, experiencing its own absence,
mourning the time when, like the moon,
I also shone with a brightness not my own.

Ann Drysdale

Risk Assessment

*Written at the request of the town council prior
to a series of poetry workshops in a local park*

The whole enterprise is fraught with hazard
When you come to think about it. No parent
Would ever let their child participate
Knowing the full extent of the danger.
Huddled for an hour in a sweaty tent
With only a poet to take care of them?
They could be inappropriately touched,
Approached by some ungodly reprobate
Offering to show them skylarks in return
For a quick peep at their budding talent.
They might catch fire; rub two ideas together
And – poof! – spontaneous creativity!
Addiction is a possibility
And the susceptible may find themselves
Unable to resist the strong compulsion
To indulge repeatedly in the habit,
For, as the wise poet wrote on the packet,
This stuff can seriously affect the heart.*

*paraphrasing Elma Mitchell – *This Poem...*

David Sutton

Immigrants

Where did they come from? From so many lands.
From mountains, jungles, deserts, snowy plains,
From regions of hot grass, from great slow rivers.
I think there was no country upon earth
That did not send these secret embassies.

Turquoise. Apricot. Mahogany.

How did they get here? In so many ways.
They came in peace and war, with song and story:
Marching in with dusty, sunburnt soldiers;
By caravan along the Silk Road; borne
In white-sailed clippers; carried on the spice wind.
None checked their coming here; no custom-house
Could hinder these that travelled light as air.

Maharajah. Sandal. Talisman.

And did we make them welcome? They were seed.
We gave them earth: some withered, some took root.
At first they tingled on our tongue, like snowflakes,
But then the strangeness melted: they were ours.

Typhoon. Anaconda. Kangaroo.

And will they come again? Never like that.
A language also has its innocence,
Its first fine careless hospitality.
Never again so multitudinous
Those migrants to our shore, like unknown birds
Alighting for the first time, opening
The proud fan of their peacock syllables.

Oleander. Lilac. Cinnamon.

Ruth O'Callaghan
Regarding Delivery.

Of course, there's no way we can guarantee
how long. The maker, normally a man,
will always believe his goods are perfect
on leaving. Difficulty may occur
in transportation, whether at departure
(particularly if the way is blocked
or when the fuel gauge is low), in transit
(the carrier may accidentally shed
the load) and even at delivery
(the packaging may skew, the goods may slip –
adopting such a difficult position
that the contractor has to use a tool
to grasp protruding parts). The cost of damage
is to be borne by the recipient.

Judy Gahagan
Autumn Charade

This autumn is a take on itself,
the ripened sun, the golden fretwork,
the day after day long swan-song for contralto

before the long quiet's strange meaning
shows; not just as winter gaping
from haggard doorways in firebombed cities

but some unimaginable devastation.
The jeremiads of warning declare
The sickness of this autumn-draped charade.

So? Yes I'll make of this morning
an organ-loft, make of it a cathedral of a morning,
its music the copper flickering and falling;

take this as it has come, stop right here.
Days live, light presences, somewhere behind the stars
allowed just once a visit to the earth

so this day comes as a copper vault and madder flares,
collage of stripped silver, batik canopies,
sun enough for a month of marigold.

I'll not think beyond this visit or make of it
a charade of conscripts, cloaked, red-haired,
smiling at some terrible hypothesis.

Connie Bensley

End Game

Those interminable games of chess...
I think it's the only reason he comes to see me.

> Those interminable games of chess.
> She always has the board out, waiting.

Generally I let him win. After all, he's come
from Chislehurst. It seems sad
to come so far for nothing
but tea and cake.

> Sometimes I try to let her win,
> but she's not much of a player.
> At least she makes a decent pot
> of Orange Pekoe.

I could be having a siesta
or catching up with my patchwork.
But that's just selfishness.

> If I made an excuse next week,
> I could get back to my notes on the Crimea.
> But she'd miss me so much.

Alan Murray
You

And like a modest party guest
who slips into the crowded room
and waits until the others leave
to tell the host she's there,

the thought of you will come to me,
out in the street or on a train,
and bide its time unnoticed
in the shadows

until, at last, alone at night,
I sense its old familiar shape
weaving through the heaving throng
of late departing worries,

and whispering: *Hush now, I'm here.*
I've been here all along.

Mercer Simpson
Honest to God

Dear God
I hope I've got
your correct address:
with so much mail
going astray these days
I wouldn't want this letter

to get lost in the post.
I hope you don't mind me
leaving the writing of it rather late
but I felt I had to write to thank you
for letting me stay in your house
for so long. I know
I haven't been the easiest of guests,
stealing your son's bread
and helping myself to his wine.
Please forgive your wayward visitor
straying into the intellectual thickets
of unbelief, of spurious questionings,
trespasser from faith's footpaths
exploring country lanes I thought
were beckoning me to Eden
which I should have known to be
forbidden territory.
Now that my time is nearly over
I insist on having the last word
which must be gratitude:
gratitude for the miracle of your world
that I, who might have died at birth,
was spared to live in;
for which I offer you my thanks
which can never be enough
for the gift of life.

So please forgive me if I seem
impertinent in asking if I may
come back and visit you again sometime?

Tim Cunningham
The Miracle Worker

It used to be so simple. You could feed
A curious five thousand with five barley loaves
And two fishes, make a neat symbolic point
And everyone was grateful. Now you get
The vegans up in arms and food fads
Sold on wheat and rye: the allergy brigade.
Magic a draught of fishes and all hell
Breaks loose about fishery allocations
And net specifications, menageries
Of 'atians as if the sea can be sliced like cake.
Rebuke the gale and lullaby the waves.
What then? Deflated surfers get the sulks,
And forecasters blame you for all their howlers.
Walk on water and you take the flak
For every drowning since old Noah's flood.
Cure a blind man with your spittle and he serves
Writs for more infections than the judge
Can spell, then claims redress for trauma
Occasioned by the ugliness all 'round.
For pity, make ten lepers clean. One
Might thank you, but the nine? The nine resent
The crowd they work with now, the office chores
And forty-hour-a-week assembly line:
Nostalgia for the bell and begging bowl.
Invite a cripple to take up his bed
And doctors blast a blunderbuss of suits,
Infest with threats, send 'psychosomatic'
Buzzing on gadfly wings. Take the next step:
Dare raise some woman's brother from the dead,
So dead that when you roll the stone 'he stinketh',
And priests proclaim you a blasphemer,

Master of the necromantic arts,
Decree that graves be shovelled six feet deep.
Tortured with texts and questions, interminably

Racked between committees and tribunals,
The poor man sits bemused, addled in extremis,
Conscious only of a blinding light
And that strange sentence: 'Lazarus, come forth!'
It gets to you. I have this premonition
Of Roman sadists crucifying some guy.
And what alarm, outcry? Friends of the Earth
With flasks and banners voicing concern about trees.

Danny Pyle

To the Edge of the Web

Held by the web of life
until reaching the outer edges
or the lines of the web
are violently shaken
by man-made explosions
and humans fall to other dimensions.
Those that make the outer edges
become frail as they age
and their tenacity weakens,
they drop into whatever
is on the other side.
But the web of life is unbroken
constantly refreshed
by more humans entering
covering our departures.

303

Rik Wilkinson

White Owl

I remember stepping from a car
                           in the early hours
Under a full December moon
                      brilliant with frost.
        Bathed in the cold beams
                    we stumbled over the courtyard,
    Our heads blanketed against the icy light.
              Under the constellations
                      and the ragged Tower

        There were owls' wings
                    and shouts of laughter
      The slamming of a car door;
    Our breath and warm voices
                    were visible in the moonlight.
At supper in the flickered kitchen
                warm conversation blazed . . .
      Then pale candles led us
                  exhausted to sleep.

        Awakened
      By the glare of the arched moon
                    crossing my sleeping
I stood by the diamond panes of the croft's
                  high window
With the moonlight crashing through the sky
                around the Tower of Shadow.
      And there at the icy glass
                    Screechowl

Suddenly spread his
                Huge wings in greeting -
Then vanished!
           And under the stares of the stars
I blushed . . . affected by so strange an honour.
   But, welcome – or omen?
                       My nape hairs
          Prickled like claws
              In the brittle silence.

Geoffrey Godbert

The Goodbye You Make In Rain

When they first met it was like
the morning when birds learn how to fly
and buds open unexpectedly;
it was like the sky and sea
coming together on a horizon
in a masterly painting
of dreams on a muslin breeze,
the sound of summer humming
from flower to flower on warm air.

The hello they made in sunshine
was infinitely curving
like a beautiful bone
and they thought this is how it's going
to be for ever and ever,
seeing each other as many
country things marvellously:
a harpsichord of rustling grass,
he said; and she, the colour of songs.

They forged their papers
with the meaning of life.
They seemed to unfold
like the place and the day.

Then shadows settled and spread
submarine darkness on the walls,
winds moved the ragged sky
in moments of nervous blue,
the trees drooped in shrugs
and twilight was a fallen dancer;
they said: let's photograph mystery
before it is too late.

I shall carry your face like spring,
he said; and she, of our heart
there is no end to its beat; they took
hands for the length of a poem,
till the star and the eyes of themselves
came close and they saw how vulnerable
things are: as he was; she was; they were.

It was like dying of memories
in solitary confinement,
a Carmelite of words
stifling love again and again
in the helpless places they had touched,
where silence was that sixth sense
of special daring not to name
the name, the cause, out loud
for fear of losing both forever.

We can kneel no more to love, he said;
and she, who will be good to us?
They took their hands in search of touch.
We can see them, glimmering
with tears, laughing a missed smile
in places of loneliness.

What is the goodbye you make in the rain?

Kathleen Kummer

When African Women Laugh

In the laughter of African women
is the silver of bells and carillons
spilling out over summery cities,

and the sound of children playing
innocent games: skimming
stones, hopscotch, skipping.

When African women laugh,
you hear rain fall on the grass
as it springs from the rust-coloured earth,

and the wind as it tugs at the washing,
filling the bright shirts as if
with their wayward husbands' bodies.

The laughter of African women
is drawn from deep down. Limpid,
it catches the sunlight, brims over,

a descending scale of well-oiled
squeaks of delight, poured
like balm on the pain of the world.

And if it is true that the flutter
of a butterfly's wings is enough
to cause a far-off disaster,

wonderful things may happen
on the other side of the planet
when African women laugh.

Mike Smith,

All Things Are Connected

Touch this web
We call the world
However lightly
With your God-finger
And see
From each concentric strand
The dew is shaken

Not one strained string
There is that does not shimmer
With that motion

Even the hollow centre
Ring of nothingness
Into which we fall
Moves

And the guy-line cables
That hold this universe in place
Tremble

Michael Swan

Joseph Never Said Much

Joseph never
said very much.
After the excitement
had all died down
he just went quietly
back to his workshop
and lined up some jobs
to keep them all fed.

Evenings after work
he used to sit
puffing his pipe
without a word
while Mary went on
about her bloody angel.

Joseph did his best
for the holy cuckoo;
tried to train him
to help in the workshop.
Frankly, the boy
wasn't very much use
(though Joseph never told him
in so many words).
He blunted the chisels
messed up the planes
and couldn't tell a dowel
from a dovetail joint.

Joseph didn't say so
but he felt a lot better
when the boy left home
and went off preaching.

And again, one Monday
some years later,
when the order came through
from the High Priest's office
for three plain crosses
by Friday morning.

Barbara Cormack

Free to Choose

When I say I love you
let it be
softly in the middle of the night
when the universe is too dazzled by itself to notice
a small new light. Or better still,
let me speak
into some empty moment of your sleep,
between dreams perhaps,
so waking you'll be free
to choose what will be dream
and what reality.

Roy Cameron

Dolphins

We had searched all day,
had scoured the waves,
the blue-black ripples,
seen through binoculars
resembling dorsal fins,
each time lifting our hearts
before dissolving them back
into the stubborn empty sea.

It was they who found us.

It was they who suddenly
announced the Mardi Gras –
a carnival parade
of shimmering outriders –
acrobats and tumblers –
too many for the eye to follow.

Easily matching our boat speed,
they came cutting across its bow,
leaping and diving,
grinning with playful curiosity
that was checking us out.

I hung low over the boat,
could almost have hitched a ride –
a youngster swam with its mother
in perfect synchronicity.
And so we moved in time and grace
                together,
raced together
through the rippling green water –

till just as suddenly
the show was over.
Like a curtain falling the rain
shifted and the sun came out
to paint a mighty arch
through which as one
the dolphins turned and left.

Danielle Hope
For January

Let me make you a present of January.
Of late sunrises, pink skies to the east –
wintry light grilling through curtains
fires in the grate, clothes from sheep.
Snow wuthers into the wind, settles on
horses stamping the fields. Thirty-one days
layered with nuts, mandarins and sleep,

I will wrap it in smeared paper, sign
with ink stained fingers. Carry it
past courtyards, verges all brown.
People tramp from work to home
back again, pass snowdrops and early
crocuses – their eyes fixed on stone.
Cherry blossom awakes the trees.

Emily Middleton

My Future

Other people live in fear
of gun massacres, heart attacks,
car smashes, plane crashes,
horrific back-street slaughters.
But me? I can tell you my future:
all two hours and twenty-six minutes of it.

I can tell you how
I will be swaddled in wires
like a new-born in a blanket;
how plastic and metal will nestle
in my flesh like vital organs.
How the firm push
in the small of my back
will feel like a mother
sending her son into the playground
on his first day of school.

I can tell you how
I will step down the path
of the grey terraced house.
How I will walk
along the pavement
clutching my belly, nursing
my newly acquired child.

I can tell you how my sweat
will mingle with dormant electrons;
how I will whisper my instructions
like a mantra as I clutch the slippery surface
of the handrail on the number 47.

I can tell you how I will
disembark deftly despite
my bulk, slip
into the crowd
as an otter
enters the water.

I can tell you how I will
murmur my final prayers,
cradling my phantom foetus;
clinging to the image
of Heaven's open gates
like a daughter to her father's hand.
How my finger will flick
the switch as the clock
tolls twelve

Tim Dooley
The Tambourica Player's Wife

His stained fingers scratched
at the sympathetic strings.
Next to him the Romany
girl was singing the usual
tales of love's abandon and
abandoned love. Songs
of freedom: with wild eyes
like the skinny cats in the
locked Serbian church.

What lines his face,
I paid for too. So when
her voice twins with his
lamenting the times, it's
my heart floods. If not for
the nation saved, for the
future he stole, the island
cottage we should have had,
the smell of cypress after rain.

Mandy Coe

Clock Mender

I know clocks want to die, all of them
working out their final breath.
But I continue to resuscitate,
demanding obedience in rounding-up
the scattered hours. I have felt the resistance

of the winding key, I know full well
the sharp-toothed ratchet that stops
a spring from spending itself with the fury
of a wasp trapped in a glass.
I enter hearts through secret doors,
oystering open watches to tease

loyalty from their core.
My magnified eye follows tweezers
fine as fishbones. The whorls of my fingertips
sparkle with salt. I see the jewelled geometry
of wheels and cogs, screws, perfect as genes;
watch-hands, small as beetle limbs.

The room is filled with ticking.
Brass pendulums cut through air,
lead weights descend on cat-gut twine.
An enamelled moon arcs behind
the sins of Adam and Eve.
A wooden bird pantomimes Spring.

Kenneth Steven

The Long Silence

On Iona the last Gaelic speaker has died.
This winter when the gales battled each roof and window
He was blown out and into the wind.

Once upon a time he was a tall man,
Leaning at the porch of his weaver's cottage,
His eyes like pools of the sea.

Now in the summer when the tourists come
You will hear the languages fast and loud –
But never a word of Gaelic there.

All over the western islands the last ones are going
Like candles tonight, falling across the wind,
Their voices drowned and lost in time.

But everyone is talking, busy talking,
The radios and televisions are loud all night,
And no-one is listening to the long silence.

Alison Chisholm

Directives

I have my instructions.
I may not water my lawn with a garden hose,
eat an apple while driving,
smoke in public.
I may not chastise my child,
and will be informed if the government
thinks he's obese.
I can be prosecuted
for failing to sort kitchen scraps from general garbage,
exceeding the speed limit,
expressing politically incorrect opinions
(even in the privacy of my own home.)
I am told how much I can drink,
how many vegetables to eat every day,
that I must cut my salt consumption.
I cannot come into contact
with any child who is not my own
unless the police have certified
that I am not a criminal.
I may not wish my neighbours a happy Christmas
in case it offends their religious beliefs.

Thank God
I live in a free country.

Sally Festing
Birthday Letters, 1994-98

Dear Auntie,

April brings the usual sun rain sun
and your first grandchild one

whole year. The photo shows her smile
Sanjay says it is similar

to his. He doesn't know
I'm writing. Speaks with his brothers, though

he feels the weight of your silence.
In your eyes he'd no licence

to marry outside the caste. It fills
you with grief, first boy & family pet broke the rules.

Please be happy, Sanjay's happiness is hard won.
I will look after your son.

Dear Auntie,

Another April! Here is Sangeetha on her bottom.
We'd like to visit you in Colombo

then you can see her for real.
Because of my troubled labour, she'll squeal

at the animals and doesn't walk.
Often we have to take her in our arms, talk

gently. A beautiful girl, people say.
She's doing so well. These are little cares of the day.

As for us, we move from one
minute to the next in surprise & expectation.

Dear Auntie,

Sangeetha is four and pushing the pram.
Vali, eighteen months, came out a little tiger.

Not all big sister's orders get obeyed!
I am well. Sanjay is frayed

because you have turned your back on him.
I'd like you to accept that things dance on the rim

of our lives over which we have little control.
To your grandchildren, your voice is a hole

in a stocking. Life will be over much too fast.
Can we unknot the past?

William Bedford

Ghosts

Only here, blackberrying,
    Are we together,
Late afternoon crisp as autumn leaves,
    Rich boughs of fruit
Heavy with a white rime,
    A frost and thinning air.

So quietly, let us walk the fields,
    Talking as if ghosts
Of a past already come,
    Like blackberries,
Darkening

Camilla Chen
Afterward

(in memory of my grandmother)

i.
How did it happen?
Ten hours and ten minutes more
but the day has ended, and I see you:
shoes still on your feet, and your clothes,
all the colours out of place against the mortuary walls.

I remember: The way you'd hold my hand
in both of yours, the way you'd ask, smiling,
Ni hao ma?

ii.
The night is eloquent
but I have hemmed myself in.

No words to give
so I fold paper and
feed it to the fire,

watching flames lick
through the petals,
each incense structure
curling and crumbling,
slowly collapsing
into ash.

I remember: Sunday afternoons at your store,
you teaching me how to count out change
and letting me sit in your storekeeper's armchair

iii.
When they sing
it's part of the ritual.
I don't understand the dialect,

your dialect, but I close my eyes
as the voices lift, soar, dip,
in a language of grief
that requires no translation.

I remember: Dinner with you,
your cooking fragrant as you urged us on,
eat, eat, eat generously, eat more.

iv.
It's a beautiful morning today
and we're sending you off.
In my head I try to talk to you,
think of the things I would have
liked to say to you, imagine
how you would have answered.

I remember: Once asking your age
and not having enough fingers and toes
for your sixty six years

v.
We watch from behind a glass panel
as you make your last journey alone,
slowly, in a box on a track, into the crematorium.

When we emerge the sky is the brightest it's been in days
I remember your smile, the creases around your eyes,
the way your hands were always cool and dry.

Nobody says a thing on the way back
But when we smile with the tears still in our eyes
I hope you know we're thinking of you.

vi.
Wai po, ni hao ma?
Wo hen hao, wo hen hao.

James Coghill

Car Crash Geography

At the end of last year
The statistician took
A map of Britain,
A ruler, a pen –
Then put a dot
Where each fatal accident
Had occurred
In the last year.

Afterwards, they joined the dots
In a veering path –
From east to west then moving up –
Until the Line slunk to the Shetlands
And disappeared.

They turned the map up on its side
Saw –
A thousand butterfly hearts
Roar –
Stabs of brakes –
The up-soar panic takes
In glass air –
The silence when
The Line in the hospital
Stops.

Rik Wilkinson

Blackbird at Twilight

I walked alone across the empty square, the traffic
momentarily silent, the air motionless, clouds lowering
on the horizon; and heard a blackbird sing from a rooftop.
His thrilling overflowed and echoed through the square.
I stood arrested – motionless – but could not stay silent;
"Yes, Blackbird – I'm listening – sing it all for me!"

And then a phrase – a magical leitmotiv – opened the portal
of a reality known only to the blackbird. A neural gateway
through which light danced and laughed . . . then instantly
closed – sealed on a realm which humankind perhaps may
glimpse, but never enter. Those fleeting notes – the pass-key
momentarily gifted by an emissary from another world.

Acknowledgements:

All the poems in this anthology first appeared in Acumen. *Many went on to appear in subsequent volumes by the individual poets and these collections are acknowledged below. Acumen would like to thank the individual poets for their permission to reproduce the poems again in an* Acumen *collection. Every effort has been made to find the copyright holders of the poems and any omissions or incorrectly assigned poems will be duly acknowledged in any further printings of this volume.*

ABBS, Peter: 'At the Extremities' was published in *Icons of Time;* Gryphon Press, 1991.
ABSE, Dannie: 'The Abandoned', 'Divorce Proceedings', 'Ghosting for Mayakovsky'and 'An Interrupted Letter' were published in *New Selected Poems;* Hutchinson, 2009.
ACHARYA, Shanta: 'After Great Struggle' was published in *Numbering Our Days' Illusions*; Rockingham Press, 1995.
ADAMS, Anna; 'The Wood Along the River's Bank' was published in *Flying Underwater;* Peterloo Poets, 2004.
ALLEN, Gary: 'Languages' was published in *Languages*; Flambard / Black Mountain Press, 2002.
ASHWORTH, Anne: 'The Far Country' was published in *The Oblique Light; poetry and peak experience;* The Quaker Universalist Group, 1988.
BAER, William: published by kind permission of the author.
BAILEY, R.V.: published by kind permission of the author.
BARDSLEY, Wendy: 'Foetus' and 'Heathcliffe' were published in *Amphitheatre;* Rockingham Press, 1996.
BARFORD, Wanda: 'About Silence' and 'Black Thomas' were published in *Losing, Finding;* Flambard, 2002.
BARKER, Sebastian: 'Linger Awhile' was published in *Damnatio Memoriae: Erased from Memory*; Enitharmon Press, 2004; 'The Sage of the Cambrian Mountains' and 'Doubletake' were published in *The Hand in the Well*; Enitharmon Press, 1996.
BARTHOLOMEW-BIGGS, Michael: 'Their Minds Were Settled' was published in *Tell It Like It Might Be;* Smokestack Books, 2007.
BEAKE, Fred; 'Signs', 'The Light', 'Burnham Beeches' and 'Elegy' were published in *New and Selected Poems;* Sheersman Books, 2006; 'Song at 51' was published in *The Cyclops;* Menard Press, 2002; 'The Light' and 'Good Men Are Gone ...' were published in *Etruscan Reader IX*, Etruscan Books, 1999; 'The Light' and 'Burnham Beeches' were published in *Places and Elegies;* University of Salzburg, 1997.
BEDFORD, William: 'Ghosts' was published in *Collecting Bottle Tops*; Poetry Salzburg, 2009.
BENSLEY, Connie: 'End Game' was published in *Private Pleasures;* Bloodaxe Books, 2007 and reproduced by kind permission of the publishers.
BENSON, Judi: 'Burying the Ancestors' was published in *Thin Places*; Rockingham Press, 2006.
BIDGOOD, Ruth: 'Characters' was published in *Singing to Wolves*, Seren, 2000.
BILLS, Gary: 'The Older World' was published in *The Echo and the Breath;* Peterloo Poets, 2001.
BORN, Anne: 'Red Wine Pantoum' was published in *Parting Light;* Headland, 1991.

BROWNJOHN, Alan: 'Throwback' was published in *The Cat Without E-Mail;* Enitharmon Press, 2001.

BURNSIDE, John: published by kind permission of the author.

BUTT, Maggie: 'Spaces' and 'Initiation' were published in *Lipstick;* Greenwich Exchange, 2007.

CAMERON, Roy: published by kind permission of the author.

CARR, Sally: 'Red Silk' was published in *Handing on the Genes;* Rockingham Press, 2003.

CARVER, Caroline: published by kind permission of the author.

CAWS, Ian: 'Wharfs' was published in *Taro Fair;* Shoestring Press, 2003; 'Clarinet' was published in *Herrick's Women;* University of Salzburg, 1996.

CHATTERJEE, Debjani: 'From the Base' was published in *Albino Gecko;* University of Salzburg, 1998.

CHEN, Camilla: published by kind permission of the author.

CHISHOLM, Alison: 'Leda's Learning' and 'Directives' were published in *Hold Tight;* Headland Publications, 2009.

CLARKE, A.C.: published by kind permission of the author.

COE, Mandy: 'Clock Mender' was published in *Clay;* Shoestring Press, 2009.

COGAN, Ross: published by kind permission of the author.

COGHILL, James: published by kind permission of the author.

COOPER, Austin: published by kind permission of the author.

COPE, Wendy: published by kind permission of the author.

CORMACK, Barbara, by kind permission of Douglas Cormack, was published in *For All Seasons;* Acumen Publications, 2009.

CORTI, Doris: published by kind permission of the author.

COTTON, John: published by kind permission of Peggy Cotton.

CROSHAW, Michael: 'A Prayer for Playing Children' and 'The Other Side of the Story' were published in *A Harmony of Lights;* University of Salzburg, 1993.

CROSS, Beryl: 'War Generations' was self-published in *A Colour that is not a Colour.*

CRUCEFIX, Martyn: 'Dolmen at Skyber Hen' was published in *An English Nazareth;* Enitharmon Press, 2004.

CUNNINGHAM, Tim: 'The Miracle Worker' was published in *Kyrie;* Revival Press, 2008.

DALE, Peter: published by kind permission of the author.

DAVIES, Hilary: published by kind permission of the author.

DAVIDS, Roy: 'White Noise', 'Silent Movie' and 'Fish' were published in *White Noise;* Acumen Publications, 2007.

DAVIS, Stella: 'Coffee in Weimar' was published in *Last Boat to Avalon;* Peterloo Poets, 2009.

DEAKIN, Julia: '20th Century' was published in *Without a Dog;* Graft Poetry, 2008.

DONAGHY, Michael: earlier versions of poems which appeared in *Collected Poems;* Picador, 2009. Published by kind permission of Maddie Paxman.

DOOLEY, Tim: 'The Tambourica Player's Wife' was published in *Keeping Time;* Salt, 2008.

DRYSDALE, Ann: 'The Case for Light Verse' and 'Risk Assessment' were published in *Between Dryden and Duffy;* Peterloo Poets, 2005.

DUNMORE, Helen: 'We are Men not Beasts' was published in *Out of the Blue: Poems*

1975 - 2001; Bloodaxe Books, 2001 and reproduced by kind permission of the publishers.

ENGLISH, June: 'Cold October' was published in *The Sorcerer's Arc;* Hearing Eye, 2004.

ENRIGHT, D.J.: published by kind permission of James Wills, Watson Little Ltd.

EWART, Gavin: published by kind permission of Margo Ewart.

FAINLIGHT, Ruth: 'Crocuses' is an earlier version of the poem published in *Moon Wheels,* 2006; 'Black' an earlier version of the poem published in *Burning Wire,* 2002. Bloodaxe Books and reproduced by kind permission of the publishers.

FANTHORPE, U.A.: 'Kinch & Lack' was published in *Consequences;* Peterloo Poets, 2000, and in *Collected Poems,* 2005. Published by kind permission of R.V. Bailey.

FARISH, Helen, published by kind permission of the author.

FESTING, Sally: published by kind permission of the author.

FISHER, Catherine: published by kind permission of the author.

FLINT, Rose: 'Women Making Bridges... ' was published in *Fire Signs;* University of Salzburg, 2004; 'Heavy Air' was published in *Mother of Pearl;* PS Avalon, 2008.

FLYNN, Stuart: 'Just Another Day in a Poet's Study' was published in *Temptation in the Desert;* Agape Publications, 2002.

FORBES, Duncan: 'Sloe Gin' was published in *Vision Mixer, 2006;* 'Moggie Thatcher' was published in *Public & Confidential, 1989;* both from Enitharmon Press.

FRENCH, Wendy: 'The Concert Pianist' was published in *Splintering the Dark;* Rockingham Press, 2005.

FRITZ, Leah: 'Yeats' was published in *Going, Going ...;* bluechrome, 2007; 'Long Distance' and 'Solstice: Winter' were published in *The Way to Go;* Loxwood Stoneleigh, 1999; 'Holiday in Les Halles' was published in *Somewhere en Route: Poems 1987-1992;* Loxwood Stoneleigh, 1992.

FULLER, Roy: 'Amatory Dreaming in Old Age' was published in *Consolations;* Secker & Warburg, 1987. By kind permission of John Fuller.

FYFE, Anne-Marie: published by kind permission of the author.

GAHAGAN, Judy: 'Unnatural Autumn' was published in *The Secret Frontiers;* Enitharmon, 2008,

GALLAGHER, Katherine: 'At Delphi' was published in *Circus Apprentice;* Arc Publications, 2006; 'Song for an Unborn' and 'Bois de Vincennes' were published in *Passengers to the City;* Hale and Iremonger, 1985.

GIOIA, Dana: 'Nocturne' was published in *Interrogations at Noon:* Greywolf Press, 2001.

GODBERT, Geoffrey: 'The Goodbye You Make in the Rain' and 'The Traveller' were published in *Collected Poems;* Poetry Monthly Press, 2007.

GREENING, John: published by kind permission of the author.

GROSS, Philip: 'Hearing Voices' was published in *Change of Address: Poems 1980 - 98;* Bloodaxe Books, 2001. Reproduced by kind permission of the publishers.

GRUBB, David H.W.: 'The Old Circus Horse' was published in *Turtle Mythologies;* University of Salzburg, 1994.

GUEST, Harry: 'A Daughter's First Term at University' was published in *A Puzzling Harvest;* Anvil Press, 2002.

GURNEY, John: 'The Acacia Tree, St. Edmund Hall, Oxford', 'Clare at Lippett's Hill' and 'Haiku' published by kind permission of Sally Gurney.

HACKETT, Joe: published by kind permission of the author.

HALL, June: 'Snakes' and 'Three Solos' were both published in *The Now of Snow;* Belgrave Press, 2004.

HAMBERGER, Robert: 'Die Bravely' was published in *The Smug Bridegroom;* Five Leaves, 2002.

HANNAH, Sophie: 'Call Yourself a Poet' was published in *The Hero and the Girl Next Door,* 1995; 'Preventative Elegy' was published in *Hotels Like Houses,* 1995; Carcanet.

HARPUR, James: 'Golden Fish' was published in *A Vision of Comets;* Anvil Press, 1993.

HARVEY, Roger: 'Lunchtime Concert: Ancient Music' was published in *Northman's Prayer;* Ulverscroft / Soundings, 1988.

HEATH-STUBBS, John: 'Ten Kinds of Birds' was published in *The Sound of LIght;* Carcanet, 1999, Published by the kind permission of Guthrie McKie.

HENRY, Michael: 'Pelion and Ossa' was published in *Panto Sphinx;* Enitharmon Press,

HERBERT W.N.: published by the kind permission of the author and Bloodaxe Books.

HESKETH, Phoebe: published by kind permission of Enitharmon Press.

HESTER, Alan: published by kind permission of the author.

HOPE, Danielle: 'The Alternative History of Jemima Puddle-Duck' and 'A Trail of Stones' were published in *Stone Ship;* Rockingham Press, 2003; 'Bad Tenant' was published in *City Fox;* Rockingham Press, 1997.

HUBBARD, Sue: 'Assimilation' was published in *Everything Begins with the Skin;* published by Enitharmon Press, 1994.

JACKSON, W.D.: 'The Gift of Tongues' was published in *Then and Now – Words in the Dark;* Menard Press, 2002.

JOHNSON, Adam: 'December 1989' and 'View from the Monument' were published in *The Spiral Staircase;* Acumen Publications, 2003; and in *Collected Poems;* Carcanet, 2004. Reproduced by kind permission of the publishers.

KAVANAGH, P.J.: 'V.E. Day' was published in *An Enchantment;* Carcanet, 1991.

KAVOUNAS, Alice: 'The Lizard' was published in *The Invited;* Sinclair Stevenson, 1995.

KENCHINGTON, Maureen: published by kind permission of the author.

KHALVATI, Mimi: 'River Sonnet' was published in *The Chine;* Carcanet 2002.

KIMBER, Eve: published by kind permission of the author.

KIRWAN, Jane: 'Looking at the River' was published in *Stealing the Eiffel Tower;* Rockingham Press, 1997.

KRAMER, Lotte: 'Exodus' was published in *Red & Black;* 2005; 'Subjunctive' was published in *The Phantom Lane;* 2000; 'Cocoon' was published in *Earthquake and Other Poems;* 1994. All from Rockingham Press.

KREITMAN, Norman: published by kind permission of the author.

KUMMER, Kathleen: published by kind permission of the author.

LEE, Lance: 'The South Sussex Downs' was published in *Becoming Human;* Author's Choice Press, 2001.

LIARDET, Tim: 'High Wire' was published in *Competing with the Piano Tuner;* Seren, 1988.

LINFORD, Mervyn: 'Talking to the Bees' was published in *Talking to the Bees;* Brentham Press, 1997.

LIVINGSTONE, Dinah: 'October 2001' was published in *Presence;* Katabasis, 2003; 'Woman in a Dressing Gown' was published in *Saving Grace;* Rivelin Grapheme, 1987.

LOYDELL, Rupert M.: 'In Real Time' was published in *The Smallest Death;* bluechrome,

2006; 'Tangerine Dream' was published in *Trajectories;* Phlebas, 1995.

LYKIARD, Alexis: 'Terminal' was published in *Judging by Disappearances;* bluechrome, 2007.

MACPHEE, Kona: 'IVF' was published in *Tails;* Bloodaxe Books, 2004. Reproduced by kind permission of the publishers.

MACKINNON, Lachlan: published by the kind permission of the author.

MAY, Julian: published by kind permission of the author.

MACPHILEMY, Kathleen: 'Redundancies' was published in *The Lion in the Forest;* Katabasis, 2004.

McADAM, Rhona: 'Sunday Driving' was published in *Cartographies;* Oolichan Books, 2006.

McFARLANE, Keith: 'Dunblane' and 'From the Window' were published in *Turning Away;* Acumen Publications, 2007.

MIDDLETON, Emily: 'My Future' was published in *Foyle Young Poets of the Year Awards;* The Poetry Society, 2006.

MOLE, John: 'The Way It Was' was published in *The Other Day;* Peterloo Poets, 2007.

MOOS, Lotte; published by kind permission of Marilyn Moos.

MOTION, Andrew: published by kind permission of the author.

MORT, Graham: 'Flowering Current' was published in *Sky Burial;* Dangaroo Press, 1989; 'The Herb Grower' was published in *A Country on Fire;* Littlewood Press, 1986.

MURRAY, Alan: published by kind permission of the author.

NEWMAN, Michael: published by kind permission of the author.

NORTH, Christopher: 'That which is Lost' was published in *A Mesh of Wires;* Smith / Doorstop, 1999.

NYE, Robert: 'Riposte' was published in *Collected Poems;* Carcanet, 1998.

O'CALLAGHAN, Ruth: 'Love Sections' and 'Regarding Delivery' were published in *Where Acid Has Etched;* bluechrome, 2007.

O'CONNELL, Richard: 'North' was published in *RetroWorlds;* University of Salzburg, 1993; 'Murderess' was published in *Dawn Crossing;* Atlantis Editions, 2003.

OSADA, Patrick: 'Twos' was published in *Short Stories: Suburban Lives;* bluechrome, 2004.

OXLEY, William: 'Just One' was published in *Sunlight in a Champagne Glass;* 2009; 'Spring Night', 'The Phoenix and the Woman', 'Horses in Winter' and 'The White Table' were published in *Reclaiming the Lyre, New and Selected Poems;* 2001. Both from Rockingham Press.

PADEL, Ruth: 'Falling' and 'The Eyes' were published in *Rembrandt Would Have Loved You;* Chatto & Windus, 1998; 'Rosa Silvestris Russica' was pubished in *Angel;* Bloodaxe Books, 1993. Reproduced by kind permission of the publisher.

PAGE, Jeremy: 'Bathing' was published in *The Alternative Version;* The Frogmore Press, 2001.

PATTEN, Brian: published by kind permission of the author.

PATERSON, Evangeline: 'Lucifer at the Fair' was published in *Lucifer at the Fair;* Stride, 1997. Published by kind permission of Peter Bennet.

PEARCE, Brian Louis: 'Oxford Movement' and 'La Belle Dame de Merci' were published in *The Proper Fuss;* University of Salzburg, 1996. Published by kind permission of Margaret Pearce.

PERMAN, David: 'Double Take' was published in *A Wasp on the Stair;* Rockingham

Press, 2004; 'Stubble Burning' and 'November 11th 1979' were published in *The Buildings;* Acumen Publications, 1997.

PETRUCCI, Mario: 'Breath' and 'Fence' were published in *Heavy Water: a poem for Chernobyl;* Enitharmon Press, 2004.

POOLE, Peggy: 'Visiting Jill' was published in *Cooee;* Driftwood Publications, 2006.

PORTER, Peter, published by kind permission of the author.

PRICE, Caroline: 'Video Games' was published in *Pictures Against Skin;* Rockingham Press, 1994.

PUGH, Sheenagh: published by kind permission of the author.

PURCELL, Sally: 'Out from the Moon's dark hillside...' was published in *Collected Poems* (ed. Peter Jay), Anvil Press Poetry 2002. Published by kind permission of the publishers.

PYLE, Danny: published by kind permission of the author.

RAINE, Kathleen: 'Honesty' was published in *The Collected Poems of Kathleen Raine;* Golgonooza Press, 2000. Published by kind permission of Brian Keeble.

REDGROVE, Peter: 'The Verderer' was published in *Into the Virgil Caverns;* Cape, 2002. Published by kind permission of Penelope Shuttle.

REID, R.T.: 'In Denial' was published in *Sacred & Profane;* Athena Press,

RUSHFORTH, Leonie: published by kind permission of the author.

RUSSELL, Peter: published by kind permission of Peter George Russell and Glyn Pursglove.

SCANNELL, Vernon: 'A Journey: A Dialogue' was published in *Behind the Lines;* Shoestring Press, 2007. Published by kind permission of Jo Peters.

SCHNEIDER, Myra: 'Leave Taking' was published in *The Panic Bird;* Enitharmon Press, 1998.

SHUTTLE, Penelope: 'Wish' and 'In All Weathers' were published in *A Leaf Out of his Book;* Carcanet Press, 1999.

SKINNER, Susan: published by kind permission of the author.

SIMPSON, Mercer: 'Honest to God' was published in *Enclosures & Disclosures,* 2007; 'Somnambulist' was published in *Early Departures, Late Arrivals,* 2006; both from Rockingham Press. Published by kind permission of Betty Simpson.

SISSON, C.H.: 'Steps to the Temple' was published in *What and Who;* Carcanet Press, 1994. Published by kind permission of J.W. Louth.

SHAPIRO, Jacqueline: published by kind permission of the author.

SMITH, Christopher J.P.: 'The Partial Resurrection of St. Medrawt Mor' was published in *Mushroom Lane;* Acumen Publications, 1997. Reproduced by kind permission of the author.

SMITH, Ken: 'In the Next Street', 'Evening Primrose' and 'Just one of you' were published in *Shed;* Bloodaxe Books, 2002. Reproduced by kind permission of Bloodaxe Books. Published by kind permission of Judi Benson.

SMITH, Mike: published by kind permission of the author.

SMITHER, Elizabeth: 'Rainbow' was published in *Red Shoes;* Random House (N.Z.), 2004; *A Question of Gravity;* Arc Publications, 2004.

SOUZA, Eunice de: published by kind permission of the author.

STAINER Pauline: published by kind permission of the author.

STANFORD, Derek: published by kind permission of Julie Stanford.

STEFFEN, Jonathan: published by kind permission of the author.

STEVEN, Kenneth: 'The Long Silence' was published in *The Missing Days;* Scottish Cultural Press, 1995.

STOREY, Edward: published by kind permission of the author.

SUTTON, David: 'At the Funeral', 'Earth to Earth' and 'The Migrants' were published in *New and Selected Poems (1965 - 2005);* Peterloo Poets, 2006.

SWAN, Michael: published by kind permission of the author.

THOMAS, R.S.: 'Match my Moments' was published in *Collected Later Poems (1988 - 2000);* reproduced by kind permission of Bloodaxe Books.

TURNER, Tony: 'Prague Lady' was published in *Belief in Something Better,* 2003; 'Where was I?' was published in *Where was I?,* 2002; both from Cherrycroft Press.

WARD, J.P.: 'Lights in the Fog' was published in *A Certain Marvellous Thing;* Seren, 1993.

WARNER, Francis: 'On Epsom Downs' was published in *Nightingales;* Colin Smythe, 1997.

WEBB, Michael: 'Cargoes' was published in *Minor Calls and Cuckoo Call;* NPF Publications, 2000.

WHITBY, Julie, published by kind permission of the author.

WHITWORTH, John: 'No Can Do' was published in *Being the Bad Guy;* Peterloo Poets, 2007,

WICKS, Susan: published by kind permission of the author.

WILKINSON, Rik: 'White Owl' and 'Blackbird at Twilight' were published in *A Hundred Mile Walk;* Acumen Publications, 2008.

WILLIAMS, Hugo: 'Alternator' and 'Everyone Knows This' were published in *Billy's Rain;* Faber & Faber, 1999.

WILLIAMS, Merryn: 'The Substitute' was published in *The Sun's Yellow Eye;* National Poetry Foundation, 1997.

WILSON, Frances: 'Widow' was published in *Rearranging the Sky,* 2004; 'The Danger of Gardens' was published in *Close to Home,* 1993; both from Rockingham Press.

WYCHERLEY, Lynne: 'Child of Stromness' was published in *North Flight;* Shoestring Press, 2006.